Stefan Wesner

Integrated Management Framework for Dynamic Virtual Organisations

Stefan Wesner

Integrated Management Framework for Dynamic Virtual Organisations

Concepts and their Application in the Data Centre

Südwestdeutscher Verlag für Hochschulschriften

Impressum/Imprint (nur für Deutschland/ only for Germany)
Bibliografische Information der Deutschen Nationalbibliothek: Die Deutsche Nationalbibliothek verzeichnet diese Publikation in der Deutschen Nationalbibliografie; detaillierte bibliografische Daten sind im Internet über http://dnb.d-nb.de abrufbar.

Alle in diesem Buch genannten Marken und Produktnamen unterliegen warenzeichen-, marken- oder patentrechtlichem Schutz bzw. sind Warenzeichen oder eingetragene Warenzeichen der jeweiligen Inhaber. Die Wiedergabe von Marken, Produktnamen, Gebrauchsnamen, Handelsnamen, Warenbezeichnungen u.s.w. in diesem Werk berechtigt auch ohne besondere Kennzeichnung nicht zu der Annahme, dass solche Namen im Sinne der Warenzeichen- und Markenschutzgesetzgebung als frei zu betrachten wären und daher von jedermann benutzt werden dürften.

Verlag: Südwestdeutscher Verlag für Hochschulschriften Aktiengesellschaft & Co. KG
Dudweiler Landstr. 99, 66123 Saarbrücken, Deutschland
Telefon +49 681 37 20 271-1, Telefax +49 681 37 20 271-0
Email: info@svh-verlag.de
Zugl.: Stuttgart, Universität Stuttgart, Diss., 2009

Herstellung in Deutschland:
Schaltungsdienst Lange o.H.G., Berlin
Books on Demand GmbH, Norderstedt
Reha GmbH, Saarbrücken
Amazon Distribution GmbH, Leipzig
ISBN: 978-3-8381-1342-5

Imprint (only for USA, GB)
Bibliographic information published by the Deutsche Nationalbibliothek: The Deutsche Nationalbibliothek lists this publication in the Deutsche Nationalbibliografie; detailed bibliographic data are available in the Internet at http://dnb.d-nb.de.

Any brand names and product names mentioned in this book are subject to trademark, brand or patent protection and are trademarks or registered trademarks of their respective holders. The use of brand names, product names, common names, trade names, product descriptions etc. even without a particular marking in this works is in no way to be construed to mean that such names may be regarded as unrestricted in respect of trademark and brand protection legislation and could thus be used by anyone.

Publisher: Südwestdeutscher Verlag für Hochschulschriften Aktiengesellschaft & Co. KG
Dudweiler Landstr. 99, 66123 Saarbrücken, Germany
Phone +49 681 37 20 271-1, Fax +49 681 37 20 271-0
Email: info@svh-verlag.de

Printed in the U.S.A.
Printed in the U.K. by (see last page)
ISBN: 978-3-8381-1342-5

Copyright © 2010 by the author and Südwestdeutscher Verlag für Hochschulschriften Aktiengesellschaft & Co. KG and licensors
All rights reserved. Saarbrücken 2010

Abstract

The trend towards Service Oriented Architecture (SOA) based distributed applications for all kind of business applications lead to a corresponding change in the Grid community. This move away from proprietary solutions and protocols for Grid applications utilizing also Web Services specifications following the SOA paradigm requires also a change of the underlying collaboration model. This model referred to as Virtual Organisation (VO) [1] was originally an almost static collaboration of rather homogeneous resource providers (such as High Performance Computing centres as realised in *Uniform Access over the Internet to Computing Resources (UNICORE)* [2] or *Distributed European Infrastructure for Supercomputer Applications (DEISA)* [3]). About ten years earlier the concept of Virtual Enterprises, Collaboration Networks, Alliances, Networks,... emerged in the economics research community [4, 5, 6, 7, 8, 9]. These concepts were not limited to the long term oriented goals associated to Grid VOs such as the support of the Large Hadron Collider experiment but targeted at a fast and efficient way to respond on market opportunities.

The starting point for this thesis was the development of a more dynamic and business oriented model for IT oriented Virtual Organisations realised by extending the rather limited understanding of Grid VOs with the dynamism of the economic models and introducing the concept of potentially dynamically agreed Service Level Agreements defining the relationship across providers and between consumer and provider(s). Beside this new model allows giving up the assumption that all VO participants agree on the overall goals of the global VO. The SLA based model allows each provider to be driven by their own business objectives and operate autonomously and independent from each other. It is also possible to provide assets to several, potentially competing, VOs at the same time.

Using this SLA driven dynamic VO model several business Grid scenarios had been analysed and classified. The classification of the scenarios led to the following abstractions:

- *Core Service Provider:* Potentially large number of providers offering quite raw services very tightly coupled to a physical resource such as data storage or computation. The offered services of the different providers can be easily compared as the number of different services is very limited.

- *Aggregated Service Provider:* Compared to the Core Service Provider the provided services are not tightly mapped on a particular physical resource but combine several core and other aggregated services to a complex, aggregated service.
- *Service Provider Collaboration:* This scenario could be built from a combination of core and aggregated service providers realising a collaboration across them e.g. with specialised roles. So one provider could be specialised on data storage, another one on providing computational services while others are realising an interface to a product database.
- *Virtual Laboratory:* This extension of the service provider collaboration scenario assumes a shared knowledge space where application designers can prepare certain applications by defining workflows or semantic rules and application users can execute them afterwards.
- *Interactive Instrument Integration:* If specific hardware such as interactive access to a radio telescopes is necessary the treatment of replaceable providers (e.g. data storage providers) and owners of unique resources need to be treated differently.

Review of existing tools and methods shows that most solutions available are pure monitoring solutions very often targeting hardware monitoring. In most cases the management of the assets is fully delegated to *technical* human operators fully decoupled from business objectives or potentially agreed SLAs. While Policy based Management (PBM) offers the right framework to realise a management also driven by SLAs and business objectives available implementations or frameworks are limited to the security domain.

Based on an analysis of the current methods and available solutions for the management of distributed applications and Grid environments a management concept addressing the requirements identified before is proposed. The management concept is organised in several layers with the idea of having different management objectives associated with each layer, use different technologies on the different layers and move from raw monitoring data more and more to business relevant information.

Each of the layers is supposed to be loosely controlled by the upper layer. The coupling is not tight as each layer should be able to operate independently and react fast. So each layer takes decisions but report them with the necessary context up the layer where decisions can be overruled or the decision basis (e.g. the rule and policy database) is updated by the higher layer.

The feasibility of the concept is demonstrated by detailing it for a service provider delivering HPC services as utilities to a dynamic virtual organisation. The presented approach splits the provider management into five management blocks. Three management blocks are performing a purely technically oriented low level management very close to the physical resources and are supported by a service management layer supporting this with a complete and integrated view. On top of this

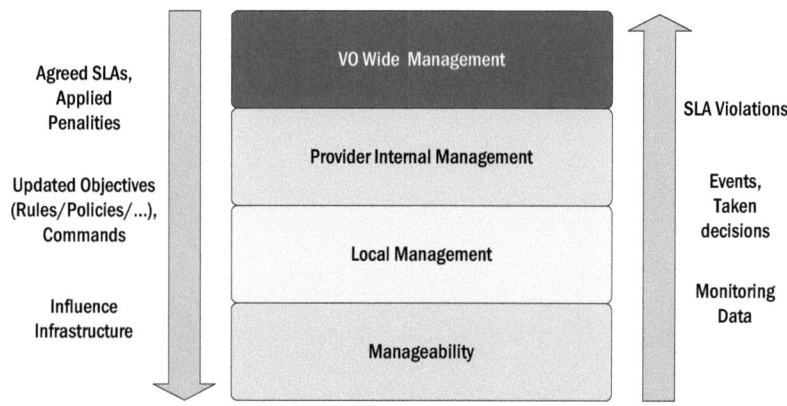

service management layer a business relation management layer is mediating between business objectives, customer relations and the technical infrastructure.

Zusammenfassung

Die zunehmende Bedeutung von Service orientierten Architekturen für kommerziell ausgerichtete verteilte Anwendungen hat sich auch auf die Ansätze im Bereich des verteilten Rechnens, dem Grid computing, ausgewirkt. Die ursprünglich ausschliefllich an den Bedürfnissen von Wissenschaftlern ausgerichteten Lösungen unter Nutzung proprietärer Protokolle und Werkzeuge sind in den letzten Jahren nach und nach unter Nutzung von Web Services realisiert worden. Neben diesen Änderungen im technologischen Bereich hat sich auch die organisatorische Struktur der Zusammenarbeit geändert. Zu Beginn wurden im Grid Bereich die *Virtuellen Organisationen* (VO) [1] als ein statischer Verbund von relativ ähnlichen Anbietern, z.B. von Höchstleistungsrechnern angesehen. Diese Art der VOs wurden unter anderem in den Projekten UNICORE [2] oder DEISA [3]) umgesetzt bis hin zum produktiven Betrieb.

Etwa zehn Jahre vor der Definition von Virtuellen Organisationen im Grid Bereich wurde bereits das Konzept von Virtuellen Firmen, Netzen oder Allianzen in der Forschung im Bereich der Betriebswirtschaft untersucht (unter anderem in [4, 5, 6, 7, 8, 9]). Diese Konzepte waren nicht an statischen und langfristigen Strukturen ausgerichtet sondern zielten vielmehr auf die kurzfristig realisierbare Zusammenarbeit von Firmen ab um möglichst schnell und effizient eine sich bietende Marktchance wahrnehmen zu können.

Der Startpunkt für die hier vorgestellte Arbeit war die Entwicklung eines dynamischeren und mehr geschäftsorientierten Modells für Virtuelle Organisation für das Grid. Dies wurde durch die Erweiterung des statischen Modells der Grid Community mit Konzepten aus den betriebswirtschaftlichen Modellen erreicht. Dieses erweiterte Modell basiert auf der Annahme, dass der Zusammenschluss von Anbietern und Nutzern dieser Leistungen nicht statisch ist und der Antrieb für das Bilden der VO nicht gemeinsame Ziele sind, sondern ökonomischen Gesichtspunkte im Vordergrund stehen. Geht man nicht mehr von der geteilten Vision aller Teilnehmer in einer VO aus ergibt sich die Notwendigkeit die Beziehungen zwischen den einzelnen Teilnehmern durch entsprechende Verträge abzusichern. Das vorgeschlagene Modell sieht vor diese Beziehungen, durch potentiell zur Laufzeit vereinbarte Dienstgütevereinbarungen, zu regulieren. Diesen Vereinbarungen legen nicht nur im Sinne eines elektronischen Vertrags die Verpflichtungen aller Vertragspartner fest, sondern enthalten ebenfalls die im Falle einer Nichterfüllung anwendbaren Maßnahmen.

Die Dokumentation der Beziehungen zwischen den einzelnen Teilnehmern einer VO durch diese Dienstgütevereinbarungen ermöglicht auch dass Dienstleistungen gleichzeitig verschiedenen VOs angeboten werden können. Dabei können die Ziele der jeweiligen VOs einander zuwiderlaufen und potentiell zu Konfliktsituationen führen bei denen ein Dienstanbieter im Falle von Engpässen bei den Ressourcen (z.B. hervorgerufen durch eine Überbuchung oder den Ausfall von Infrastruktur) nicht alle Vereinbarungen einhalten kann.

Unter Nutzung dieses dynamischen VO Modells wurden mehr als zwanzig Grid Szenarien aus verschiedenen europäischen Forschungsprojekten wie TrustCoM, GRASP, NextGrid und BEinGRID hauptsächlich aus dem Bereich Grid computing untersucht. Da das Ziel dieser Arbeit nicht ein Management Konzept für ein bestimmtes Szenario ist, sondern die Realisierung eines allgemeinen Ansatzes, wurden die Szenarien mit dem Ziel analysiert typische Muster von Grid Szenarien mit einem kommerziellen Hintergrund zu extrahieren. Dabei wurden die folgenden Szenarien erarbeitet:

- *Basisdienstanbieter:* Unter diese Klasse fallen Anbieter die Dienstleistungen anbieten die relativ stark mit der darunterliegenden Hardware verbunden sind. Ein typisches Beispiel dazu wäre das Anbieten von Rechenleistung oder Speicherkapazität. Die Besonderheit in diesem Fall ist, dass es zu erwarten ist, dass die verschiedenen Anbieter relativ leicht zu vergleichen sind und die Dienste in sehr ähnlicher, im besten Fall sogar standardisiert anbieten können. Dieser Art von Anbietern fällt es sehr schwer sich von anderen ähnlichen Anbietern abzugrenzen insbesondere weil das Know-how zur Realisierung von komplexen Dienstleistungen auf Basis dieser Grunddienste beim Anwender liegt.

- *Anbieter zusammengesetzter Dienste:* Im Vergleich zu den bereits besprochenen Basisdienstanbietern wird hier durch Kombination von Diensten ein komplexerer Dienst zusammengesetzt. Diese Aggregation von Grunddiensten und potentiell auch anderen zusammengesetzter Dienste ermöglicht eine deutlich bessere Abgrenzung zu konkurrierenden Anbietern und die effektive und effiziente Zusammenstellung stellt ein besondere Fähigkeit des Anbieters dar, die auch zu Abgrenzung zu konkurrierenden Anbietern genutzt werden kann.

- *Kollaboration:* Diese Szenario kombiniert die Basisdienstanbieter mit den Anbietern komplexer Dienste in einer Zusammenarbeitsstruktur. Eine solche Struktur bringt verschiedene Anbieter zusammen, da verschiedene Dienstleistungen benötigt werden um zu einer Lösung zu gelangen. Ein einfaches Beispiel wäre die Kollaboration eines Basisdienstleisters für Rechenleistung und einem externen Lizenzgeber der die notwendigen Lizenzen für die Nutzung einer Anwendungen bereitstellt.

- *Virtuelles Labor:* Virtuelle Labore sind eine Erweiterung des Kollaborationskonzeptes. Zusätzlich wird nicht nur von einer Art Anwender ausgegangen sonder einer Rollenteilung eines *Application Designers*, welcher die Kollaboration aufsetzt und dem *Application User* zum Beispiel vorgefertigte Arbeitsabläufe definiert welcher dieser dann zu einem späteren Zeitpunkt ausführen kann.

- *Interactive Instrument Integration:* Eine weitere Besonderheit ist die Integration von essentiellen Ressourcen die nur von einem bestimmten oder nur sehr wenigen Anbietern bereitgestellt werden können. Sind manche Anbieter, wie zum Beispiel für das Speichern von Daten, leicht austauschbar lassen sich andere Ansätze im Falle schlechter Leistung verfolgen, als dies mit einem Anbieter einer essentiellen Ressource möglich ist.

Ein Vergleich der Anforderungen dieser Szenarien mit bestehenden Ansätzen zur Überwachung von verteilten Anwendungen oder Grids zeigt dass diese meist reine Lösung zur Sammlung von Daten sind. Darüber hinaus werden häufig reine Hardwaredaten gesammelt die nicht ohne weiteres auf das Einhalten von extern zugesagten Dienstgütevereinbarungen abgebildet werden können. Typischerweise wird die Überwachung von Ressourcen nur an technischen Gesichtspunkten ausgerichtet. Eventuell definierte Ziele des Unternehmens oder potentielle negative Auswirkungen durch das Verletzen von Dienstgütevereinbarungen werden nicht berücksichtigt. Diese Beobachtung ist nicht überraschend wenn man berücksichtigt dass viele dieser Lösungen für eScience Infrastrukturen entworfen sind, in denen kommerzielle Aspekte nicht relevant sind.

Basierend auf der Analyse bestehender Lösungen und den Anforderungen aus den untersuchten Szenarien wird ein hierarchisches Management Konzept vorgeschlagen. Jeder dieser Stufen operiert zu großen Teilen unabhängig und ist für die jeweilige Aufgabe spezialisiert. Dabei erfolgt die Kopplung der verschiedenen Stufen über einen Nachrichtenaustausch über getroffene Entscheidungen von unteren hin zu höheren Stufen und umgekehrt können höhere Stufen an niedrigere Stufen Kommandos weiterleiten. Eine spezielle Möglichkeit für ein Kommando ist die Aktualisierung der Wissensbasis. Durch eine Änderung der Wissensbasis (zum Beispiel für reguläre Betriebszustände) kann das jeweilige Verhalten verändert werden.

In der obigen Abbildung ist das Konzept dargestellt dass ausgehend von Informationen die auf der Ebene der ausführenden Hardware und Softwareinfrastruktur gesammelt werden die Information mehr und mehr auf die Ebene von Dienstgütevereinbarungen gebracht werden. Auf der anderen Seite sieht das Konzept eine klare Entscheidungshierarchie vor bei dem die Geschäftsziele ausgedrückt in den vereinbarten Dienstgüten die technischen Management Stufen steuern. Diese grundlegende Konzept wird weiter verfeinert und schlägt eine Architektur zur Realisierung von Management Blöcken vor und wie diese miteinander gekoppelt werden sollen. Ein besonderer Aspekt ist die Grenze des Anbieters an der ein sogenannter *Mediator* vorgeschlagen wird, der

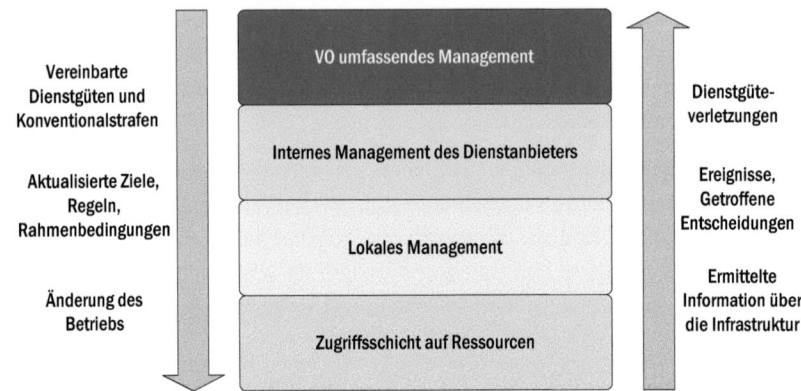

zum Einen die notwendige Transformation von Nachrichten im Anbieter internen Format mit denen im VO weiten Format leistet und zum Anderen als Filter von Nachrichten dient da nicht alle Information allen externen Entitäten zur Verfügung gestellt werden können.

Die Anwendbarkeit dieses Konzeptes wird am Beispiel eines Anbieters von Rechenleistung gezeigt in dem die allgemeinen Konzepte verfeinert werden und die jeweiligen Abläufe auf den verschiedenen Stufen dargelegt werden. Der gewählte Ansatz für das Beispiel basiert auf drei Stufen. Die unterste Stufe mit der Aufgabe ein Management der Hardware und grundlegender Softwarekomponenten zu realisieren basiert auf einem regelbasiertem Management um schnelle Entscheidungen für Gegenmaßnahmen möglich zu machen. Die nächste Stufen hat die Aufgabe die Gesamtheit aller Dienste zu überwachen und dient als Bindeglied zwischen dem Hardware orientierten Management Layer und der obersten Ebene die sich um das Management der Geschäftsbeziehungen kümmert. Auf dieser obersten Ebene werden die angebotenen Dienstgütevereinbarungen verwaltet und eine Priorisierung der parallel aktiven Vereinbarungen durchgeführt. Die Priorisierung erfolgt auf der Basis von Daten über die Kunden und dem sich aus dem Schaden bei Nichterfüllung ergebenden Risiko.

Contents

1 **Introduction and Rationale**   1
    1.1 Objectives 3
    1.2 Chosen Approach 3
    1.3 Research Contribution 4
    1.4 Background 6

2 **A new Taxonomy for Virtual Organisations**   7
    2.1 Applications spanning across several Organisations 7
    2.2 Existing Virtual Organisation Models 8
    2.3 A proposed more sophisticated VO Model 9
       2.3.1 Structural and Organisational Properties of a Virtual Organisation 10
             2.3.1.1 Topologies 13
       2.3.2 Role Model 16
             2.3.2.1 Dynamic Virtual Organisation Roles 17
             2.3.2.2 Service Provider Domain 18
             2.3.2.3 User Domain 20
             2.3.2.4 Trusted Third Party 22
       2.3.3 Dynamic Viewpoint 23
             2.3.3.1 Identification 25
             2.3.3.2 Formation 25
             2.3.3.3 Operation 26
             2.3.3.4 Evolution 27
             2.3.3.5 Termination 27

3 **Classification of Scenarios and Derived Requirements**   29
    3.1 The Method for the Scenario Classification 29
    3.2 Core Service Provider Scenario 30
       3.2.1 Topological View 31

	3.2.2	Dynamic View	32
	3.2.3	Key Requirements summary	33
3.3	Aggregated Service Provider Scenario		35
	3.3.1	Topological View	35
	3.3.2	Dynamic View	35
	3.3.3	Key Requirements summary	36
3.4	Service Provider Collaboration		38
	3.4.1	Topological View	39
	3.4.2	Dynamic View	40
	3.4.3	Key Requirements summary	42
3.5	Virtual Laboratories		44
	3.5.1	Topological View	45
	3.5.2	Dynamic View	45
	3.5.3	Key Requirements summary	46
3.6	Interactive Instrument or Simulator Integration		47
	3.6.1	Topological View	47
	3.6.2	Dynamic View	47
	3.6.3	Key Requirements summary	48
3.7	Context dependent Applications		49
	3.7.1	Key Requirements summary	50
3.8	Analysis Summary		50

4 State of the Art and Relevant Standards 53

4.1	Core Technologies			53
	4.1.1	Service Oriented Architecture		53
	4.1.2	Grid computing		55
		4.1.2.1	UNICORE	56
		4.1.2.2	Globus Toolkit	58
		4.1.2.3	gLite	59
		4.1.2.4	Grid based Aggregated Service Provision	59
		4.1.2.5	Grid for Industrial Applications	60
4.2	Information Models and Management Protocols			61
	4.2.1	GLUE		61
	4.2.2	SNMP		61
	4.2.3	DMI		62
	4.2.4	CMIP		63

	4.2.5	CIM	63
	4.2.6	MIMO	64
	4.2.7	Grid Monitoring Architecture	64
		4.2.7.1 R-GMA	64
		4.2.7.2 Web Service Level Agreements	65
		4.2.7.3 Generic System Supervision	66
		4.2.7.4 Management using Web Services (MUWS)	67
		4.2.7.5 Web Based Enterprise Management	68
		4.2.7.6 Nagios	68
		4.2.7.7 Ganglia	69
		4.2.7.8 Lemon	69
		4.2.7.9 INCA	70
		4.2.7.10 GridICE	71
	4.2.8	Tivoli	72
	4.2.9	Unicenter (Computer Associates)	72
	4.2.10	Openview (HP)	72
	4.2.11	Openmaster (Evidian-Bull)	72
4.3	Existing Management Approaches		73
	4.3.1	Rule based Approaches	73
	4.3.2	Policy Based Management	74
4.4	Summary and Conclusions		75

5 Monitoring and Management Concepts — 79

5.1	Concepts and Terminology		79
5.2	Conceptual View		81
	5.2.1	Manageability Layer	82
		5.2.1.1 Integrated Sensor	83
		5.2.1.2 Indirect Sensor	83
		5.2.1.3 Aggregation and Integration	84
		5.2.1.4 Sensor Cache and History	85
		5.2.1.5 Command Enforcement	85
		5.2.1.6 Resource Delegate	86
	5.2.2	Provider Internal Management Layers	86
		5.2.2.1 Data/Event Receiver	88
		5.2.2.2 Enactor	88
		5.2.2.3 Command Sender	90

		5.2.2.4	Local Management Layer	90
		5.2.2.5	Provider Boundary Management Layer	90
	5.2.3	VO Management layer		91
5.3	Key Building Blocks			93

6 Application of the Concept — 103
6.1 HPC computing utility provider — 103
    6.1.1 Realising the Manageability Layer — 106
    6.1.2 Local Management — 107
    6.1.3 Service Management — 110
        6.1.3.1 Report Categorization and Evaluation — 110
        6.1.3.2 Decision Module — 112
        6.1.3.3 Mapping Decisions to Commands — 114
        6.1.3.4 Rule updates and Command Reception — 116
    6.1.4 Business Relations — 116
    6.1.5 Mediation Component — 120
6.2 Operational Considerations — 120

7 Conclusion and Outlook — 123
7.1 Future work — 124
    7.1.1 Modelling Support to feed the various Knowledge Bases — 124
    7.1.2 Supporting coupled applications on hybrid computing systems — 125
    7.1.3 Standardisation of Incident Reports and Command formats — 126
    7.1.4 Cross-layer communication and self-organizing approaches — 127

Bibliography — 129

Abbreviations — 143

List of Figures

1.1 Approach in Event driven process chain notation as defined in [10] 5
2.1 High level view of a virtual organisation 11
2.2 Topology for Hub-and-Spoke and Broker scenarios 14
2.3 Topology for the peer to peer structure 15
2.4 Sample topology for the chained structure 15
2.5 Coarse grained view on the roles and their relations in the service provider domain . 17
2.6 Coarse grained view in role interactions from the User Domain viewpoint 21
2.7 Conceptual model and design and implementation of virtual organisation according to Katzy in [11] 23
2.8 Proposed Lifecycle Model for Dynamic Virtual Organisations 26

3.1 Sample Building Blocks of the Core Service Provider Scenario 31
3.2 Topological View on the Core Service Provider Scenario 32
3.3 The Service Provider view of the Collaborative Engineering Scenario 39
3.4 Example setting of the space simulation scenario 49

4.1 Basic concept of the Service Oriented Architecture 54
4.2 UNICORE architecture 57
4.3 GRIA fundamental architecture 60
4.4 GMA compound producer and consumer concept 65
4.5 MUWS Architecture 68
4.6 The Ganglia architecture [12] 69
4.7 The Lemon and FDR concept [13] 70
4.8 The GridICE layered architecture according to [14] 71
4.9 Layered approach of policy based management 74

5.1 Conceptual View of the Management Framework 81
5.2 a simple monitoring scenario 84
5.3 Simplified management flow for the web server farm scenario 87

List of Figures

5.4	message types on the different layers	91
5.5	Concept for the realisation of all management blocks in the hierarchy	96
5.6	Chaining concept for the internal management	98
5.7	boundary management	99
5.8	VO Management block	100
6.1	Deployment view of the services for the HPC utility provider	104
6.2	Chosen layers and their relations	105
6.3	Data collection for the System and Network Layer	107
6.4	Activities for the Local System and Network Management	108
6.5	Update of the Rules Datastore	109
6.6	DataReceiver component for the Service Management Layer	111
6.7	Activity flow for the decision process	113
6.8	Activity flow for reliable command sending	115
6.9	Activity flow triggered by the availability of a new SLA	119
6.10	Roles and Use Cases	122
7.1	Knowledge Engineering Approach	125

List of Tables

2.1	Structural properties of Virtual Organisations	13
2.2	Lifecycle of a Virtual Organisation	24
3.1	Dynamic View for the Core Service Provider Scenario	33
3.2	Dynamic View for the Aggregated Service Provider Scenarion	36
3.3	Dynamic View for the Multiple Service Provider Scenario	42
3.4	Dynamic View for the Virtual Laboratory Scenario	46
3.5	Dynamic view for scenarios with special or unique resources	48
4.1	Requirements mapped on available standards and technologies	77
5.1	Definition of used terms	80
5.2	Anticipated typical methods and corresponding decision times	94
6.1	SLAs for the HPC utility provider case	118

List of Tables

Chapter 1

Introduction and Rationale

The availability of the Internet as a utility has lead to several emerging trends around the general move from monolithic to distributed cross-organisational applications. The first trend is to aim for a complete *virtualisation* of resources and hide heterogeneity of an IT infrastructure such as computational and data storage infrastructures. Recently this has been further developed to a wider set of resource types ranging from physical resources such as network, computation and data toward a more general understanding including application, information and knowledge resources. Along with these developments the concept of service provision of resources as an utility not only within one organisation but also across organisational boundaries has emerged in several application domains. Based on these fundamental trends toward virtualisation of resources and services the notion of composed services that combine these utilities to complex services e.g. driven by a business process description or pre-defined bundles lead to new kind of applications that are no longer built as a monolithic block but are highly configurable and adaptable to changing conditions and environments. Beside the composition on service level also organisational boundaries need to be considered if the composed services are owned and controlled by different entities. Collaboration across organisational boundaries, also known as a Virtual Organisation (VO) [1] is one of the key concepts adopted by the Grid community. Initial models targeted at VOs built from a very small number of organisations with a low number of different service types such as compute services or data storage access. A typical example are the Virtual Organisations of virtual computing centres realised in research projects such as *Uniform Access over the Internet to Computing Resources (UNICORE)* [15], *Distributed European Infrastructure for Supercomputer Applications (DEISA)* [3] and *Enabling Grids for E-Science (EGEE)* [16]. More dynamic, business process driven Virtual Organisations are currently under research in several European research projects in the domain of eBusiness and Next Generation Grids such as *TrustCoM*[1] [17, 18], *NextGrid*[2] [19] and

---

[1]http://www.eu-trustcom.com
[2]http://www.nextgrid.org

Akogrimo[3] [20, 21, 22]. It is important to outline that distributed applications of this type are in contrast to developments in the domain of metacomputing [23] not aiming to realise a rather tight coupling of the resources and exchange of information messages with low latencies but following the paradigm of a Service Oriented Architecture (SOA) where different services are expected to be loosely coupled and exchangeable at runtime. Another important differentiator to tightly coupled systems driven mainly by performance is the role of economics as indicator if and how a collaboration is established. This means that the selection of a collaboration partner is not only based on the technical and functional properties offered by a service provider but also on properties like reputation, price and guaranteed service levels. It is important to note that service levels are not necessarily limited to Quality of Service (QoS) but a Service Level Agreement (SLA) is more seen as an electronic form of a contract between service consumers and providers. Next Generation Grid Systems as defined in [24] or the Web Services community is following this trend of Service Based Infrastructures (SBI).

The underpinning technologies of this organisational changes are the adoption of component technology and the paradigm of SOA. The most successful realisation of the SOA paradigm are Web Services [25] that will according to [26] play a major role in IT starting from 2006 and are integral part of several standard application frameworks such as the .NET framework or open source solutions such as the Axis Toolkit[4]. Additionally many commercial products of all major IT vendors do exist.

However the problem of a successful supervision of the operation of these kind of distributed applications is not solved. Distributed applications require the availability and responsiveness of resources across organizational and security domains. Many distributed systems still run in 'best-effort' mode without or sufficient monitoring mechanism on the availability and quality of the resources involved in the distributed scenario. This operation mode is not applicable for commercial settings where resources are either accounted or a Service Level Agreement (SLA) toward the customer must be fulfilled. This is not only applicable for e-commerce or Application Service Provision (ASP) solutions but especially in the scientific and engineering domain where the requirements on Quality of Service on all levels from hardware over network to application resources are high. In order to guarantee the successful operation of distributed applications the status of resources must be analysed before the application is started, during the operation phase and also after the application is finished.

Another problem of traditional monitoring solutions is their focus on networking and topologies that changes infrequently. With concepts like the Grid, especially with the introduction of dynamic

---
[3] http://www.mobilegrids.org
[4] http://ws.apache.org/axis/

Virtual Organisation (VO) (as described above), new solutions that automates the deployment, control and execution of necessary operational boundaries and policies for example Service Level Agreement and Service Level Objectives (SLO) must be defined.

1.1 Objectives

The monitoring of resources such as network routers using e.g. Simple Network Management Protocol (SNMP) and Management Information Base (MIB) or computers using technologies such as the Windows Management Interface (WMI) for the Windows Operating System based on the Component Information Model (CIM) standard is easily possible and well understood. However the simple collection of the status of involved resources in a distributed system is not sufficient.

The objective of this thesis is to rely on the existing results in monitoring and well defined information models to derive an integrated framework enabling the *management* of dynamic virtual organisations for a wide range of different scenarios. Starting from a new VO model based on the model emerged within the Grid community amended with results from the research activities in the field of economics the proposed model assumes that all relationships between providers and between consumer and provider is controlled by Service Level Agreements. These SLAs are driving the management activities within the service provider and consumer domain but respect the fact that the owner of resources want to maintain the full control over their assets. This approach allows a decoupled management for each provider/consumer independently from the goals or structure of the Virtual Organisation. As a second result this allows also the participation in several Virtual Organisations at a time with the same set of resources.

1.2 Chosen Approach

The starting point for this thesis is the assumption that the existing VO models in the Grid community with their centralized and static viewpoint are not suitable for an application in commercial oriented scenarios. In this scenarios no centralized control but a more loosely coupled collaboration of mostly independent and autonomous entities is assumed. Consequently the existing tools for the control and management of Virtual Organisations are insufficient.

The first step taken (as shown in figure 1.1) was to develop a new VO model by amending the existing VO models in Grids with research results from the field of economics. This extended, Service Level Agreement (SLA) oriented model, is no longer based on static coalitions of rather homogeneous providers but assumes a loosely coupled and dynamic relationship among them.

Chapter 1 Introduction and Rationale

The analysis of Grid use cases and other distributed applications from a couple of European research projects utilizing this VO model lead to a classification of the scenarios as a set of 'typical cases'. For these cases the key requirements for a management solution have been worked out.

The review of existing work and these key requirements has been used as input for a gap analysis identifying missing functionality. The next step was to derive from the requirements, the gap analysis results and other related work a layered model and an overall management concept. The validation of the concept is realised by an instantiation in the domain of High Performance Computing (HPC).

The thesis is concluded with a summary of the results, potential applications of the framework in other domains and proposed future research directions.

1.3 Research Contribution

The research contribution of this work is a new taxonomy for Virtual Organisations amending the rather limited Grid VO model with results from the research community in economics and using this taxonomy for a classification and requirements elicitation for business grid scenarios. The author and others have published these concepts [27, 28, 18, 21, 29, 17] and variations and refinements of the presented model have emerged in the last years and can be seen as widely accepted within the business oriented grid research community.

The major result is an integrated and layered management architecture for such Virtual Organisations. The model is assuming an Service Level Agreement (SLA) driven collaboration across providers and between consumer and provider and is instantiated in the domain of High Performance Computing (HPC). The concept is based on the work of the author as lead architect of the GeneSyS project and has been published by the author and others in [30, 31, 32, 33, 34].

In summary the major contributions of this thesis are as follows:

1. A new taxonomy for Virtual Organisation far beyond existing models in the Grid community integrating research results on Virtual Organisations from the field of economics towards an Service Level Agreement (SLA) driven dynamic collaboration model.

2. An integrated management concept for such Virtual Organisations considering business aspects as well as technical constraints and re-use of existing tools.

3. An instantiation of the framework for an HPC utility provider as a layers approach and detailing the activity flow for each of them.

1.3 Research Contribution

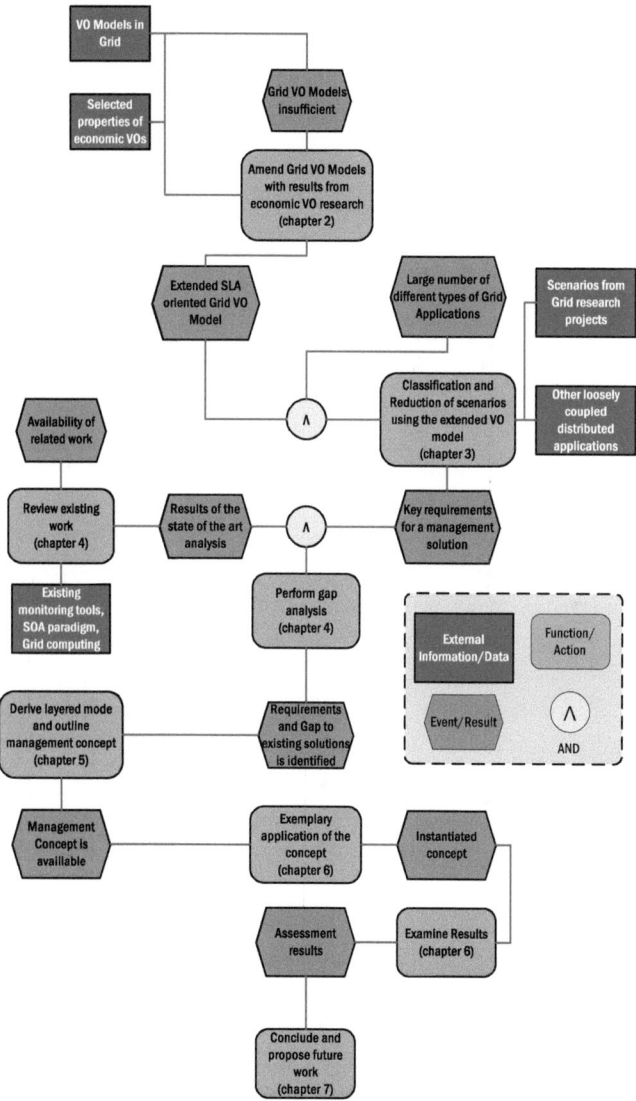

Figure 1.1: Approach in Event driven process chain notation as defined in [10]

Beside these major results this work also contains an analysis of existing approaches for monitoring of distributed applications and a comparison of passive monitoring approaches where the management of the systems is done by a human operator and more automated supervision or management systems and a gap analysis.

In general the results had been intentionally not tightly coupled with a programming language, an operating system or even a specific realisation of the Service Oriented Architecture paradigm. While as of now only Web Services seems to be a available as a decently elaborated Service Oriented Architecture platform the presented framework only assumes that the different organisations, or more precisely the services offered by them, are loosely coupled and following open interfaces and protocols.

1.4 Background

The research performed by the author as lead architect of the research project *Generic System Supervision (GeneSyS)* built the basis for the more comprehensive management framework approach presented here. As part of *GeneSyS* a Generic Supervision Architecture for distributed systems has been developed. This architecture provide components for the collection of performance data on different levels from hardware over network up to services, components and applications and has been validated in several application contexts such as distributed training and web server monitoring. The solution realised for supporting human operators and did not contain any automation or dynamic settings. Furthermore the assumption taken was that the different organisations involved in the distributed application are connected by secure channels and participate only in one application at a time.

Within the research project *Grid based Application Service Provision (GRASP)* basic Service Level Agreement (SLA) Monitoring services for Application Service Provision applications utilizing Grid has been developed as part of the work of the author within the research project and an initial integration of SLAs into Virtual Organisations has been considered. The solution developed was limited to the quite simple provision of computing resources for pre-defined application services.

Furthermore the requirements analysis for dynamic distributed applications conducted as part of the work in the Integrated Projects *Trust and Contract Management Framework (TrustCoM), European Learning Grid Infrastructure (ELeGI), Business Experiments in Grids (BEinGRID)* and *Access to Knowledge through the Grid in a Mobile World (Akogrimo)* has been exploited in particular in chapter 3.

Chapter 2

A new Taxonomy for Virtual Organisations

This work targets scenarios where the application is built from several services delivered by different organisations. While the framework can handle also simpler cases e.g. a simple client server scenario the overhead of the management framework would not be justified.

This chapter is seen as the first step towards the definition of the framework and will be a key element to motivate the chosen building blocks of the management framework described in chapter 5.

Starting from a definition of cross organisational applications a definition of Virtual Organisation is developed from different viewpoints. The proposed new taxonomy combine ideas from different domains most notably Grid Computing, Collaborative Working environments and from the economic disciplines of Enterprise Networks, Outsourcing and Virtual Enterprises. The description of conceptual roles expected in such a dynamic Virtual Organisation are briefly outlined. The chapter is concluded by the dynamic viewpoint on Virtual Organisations in the form of a lifecycle model. This model is used in the next chapter to identify specific requirements for each of the phases for all scenarios.

2.1 Applications spanning across several Organisations

The application scenarios described in chapter 3 are of very different nature and complexity in order to deliver a broad range of requirements. However the clearly most challenging applications are built from services delivered by different organisational entities. This can be different companies or units within a company that are managed independently. In this thesis obviously not

Chapter 2 A new Taxonomy for Virtual Organisations

all aspects of cross organisational applications can be tackled. As outlined in section 1.4 the presented work is aligned with ongoing European research projects and will rely on their decisions and solutions not directly relevant for the management framework. For example the anticipated framework is not intended to propose specific solutions for cross organisational identity management, dynamic security or reputation management. This consequently requires that the scenarios will not be analysed in depth with respect to properties out of scope for the management. For example security requirements will only analysed if relevant for the management framework.

A cross organisational distributed application for this work is defined as

> ...an application that is built from at least two services that need to exchange messages potentially through an uncontrolled communication channel to deliver and are managed independently by different organisational entities. Such applications might evolve over time and certain entities with their services might be added or removed.

The most important aspect is that the different organisational entities are connected via a communication channel controlled by one or more third parties (e.g. delivery guarantee, certain service levels, ...) and both entities are operating independently. This does not mean that they are not communicating to agree or negotiate behaviour or align their management decisions but there is not necessarily a central entity that can *impose* a certain behaviour.

2.2 Existing Virtual Organisation Models

There is no universally accepted generic model for a Virtual Organisation (VO). In the late 90s the concept of Virtual Organisations or Corporations, also referred to as Networks [4, 7, 8, 9] or Alliances [5, 6] emerged in the domain of economics as an organisational management level model where several companies integrate business processes across organisational boundaries. Additional to this structural view for an established Virtual Organisation a process oriented view discussing the dynamics for building and terminating a Virtual Organisation have been considered for example in [7, 11, 35]. Beside in [36] a model integrating this structural and process oriented view is presented.

Byrne defines in [4] a Virtual Organisation as follows:

> ...a virtual organization is a temporary co-operation of independent companies - suppliers, customers, even erstwhile rivals – linked by information technology to share skills, costs, and access to one another's markets...

The Grid community defines a Virtual Organisation as a mechanism for controlled resource sharing [1]. While adopting the Service Oriented Architecture (SOA) paradigm and the move from computational and data grids towards the information and knowledge Grid, also labelled as Next Generation Grids (NGG), the understanding of Virtual Organisations developed in [37, 38] to this rather unspecific description:

> ... an abstraction for resource sharing and collaboration action across multiple administrative domains...

As a result the Grid community has a rather well defined model for a Virtual Organisation for first generation, infrastructure oriented grids such as implemented in UNICORE [15, 39, 2], DEISA [3] or EGEE [16] . These models are rather static in its nature and are not created based on a business demand or opportunity but are intended to be established as an infrastructure for a large scientific community.

2.3 A proposed more sophisticated VO Model

Next Generation Grid research projects that are not targeting purely the eScience community but are also open to commercial application of Grid technology are demanding more dynamic or agile Virtual Organisation Models as shown by the author and others in [17, 18, 40, 41]. In [27] the author and others have presented a first definition of such Virtual Organisations based on an earlier definition from the TrustCoM project [42] as follows:

> A Virtual Organization (VO) is understood as a temporary or permanent coalition of geographically dispersed individuals, groups, organizational units or entire organizations that pool resources, capabilities and information to achieve common objectives. Virtual Organizations can provide services and thus participate as a single entity in the formation of further Virtual Organizations. This enables the creation of recursive structures with multiple layers of *virtual* value-added service providers.

The following subsections will further detail this definition of a Virtual Organisation from different viewpoints. First the general principles of a Virtual Organisation are discussed and different structures and organisational models are presented. The second viewpoint discusses the Virtual Organisation by looking at actors and roles. The last part looks at the dynamics involved with Virtual Organisations and the associated lifecycle and the specific tasks with a particular focus on the challenges for the management of distributed systems.

2.3.1 Structural and Organisational Properties of a Virtual Organisation

A Virtual Organisation is built from at least two legal organisations that are acting as resource or service provider. Sharing a resource can only be done if a set of functionalities are provided to use and operate them. In literature very often the term resource is used as a reference to a service for a real physical resource whereas the term service is seen as a more abstract concept composed via a combination of physical resources. In this document the latter definition is used. The major pre-condition is that there must be an agreement between these two companies to share resources under certain conditions (which do not mean that these resources are provided free of charge). Furthermore these resources may be provided at the same time to more than one Virtual Organisation (this basic principle is shown in figure 2.1). The assumption that a resource is not provided exclusively to one Virtual Organisation and that in consequence a resource owner must fulfil at the same time several, potentially competing or even contradictory requirements leads to the following fundamental implications:

- A Virtual Organisation needs to be managed. This cannot be done on global or VO wide level, but *must* be done in a decentralised fashion (see also [43]).
- Some VO members may be replaceable, some others may provide a unique type of service or resource.
- The potentially conflicting interests of the resource owner and the other collaborators in the Virtual Organisation must be managed and ensured by means e.g. of an electronic contract not only documenting the agreed service quality and conditions, but also measures to be taken in case of violation of them.
- The organisational structure of the Virtual Organisation has significant impact on how the potentially high number of organisations participating are configured, how the contracts are established and negotiated and in which way the management of the distributed system is divided between an entity on VO level and a management system on service provider level.
- There might be only one partner in the VO that interacts with the customer and may act as prime contractor or core partner.

It is important to mention that some of these assumptions are in contradiction to the VO model applied in major Grid deployments such as *Enabling Grids for E-Science (EGEE)* [16] or *Distributed European Infrastructure for Supercomputer Applications (DEISA)* [3]. The respective management solutions are operating across organisations on a VO wide level and do not consider actively competing interest for the resources provided to the VO. The assumption mentioned above that the

2.3 A proposed more sophisticated VO Model

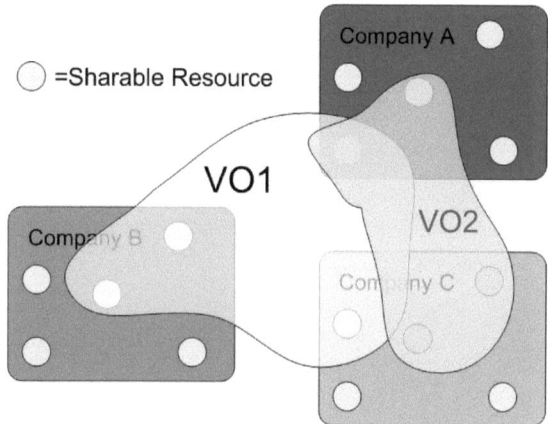

Figure 2.1: High level view of a virtual organisation

management can only be done by the resource owners also include the potential risk that a resource owner is *intentionally* not providing the resource according to the agreed contract. The resource owner may have based such a decision on an internal prioritisation of several competing consumers of the resource. This prioritisation could be based on importance of the service (e.g. an emergency service) or economic considerations (industrial client or more expensive interactive service).

The properties of a Virtual Organisation are summarised in table 2.1. The structure of this table is inspired by the table presented in [36] on page 6–7.

Property	Definition
Goal Specific	The Virtual Organisation is built to achieve a specified goal. Each participant is providing a contribution towards this goal
Formalised	The co-operation among the participants is formulated in the form of electronic contracts in which the behaviour and roles are explicitly formulated and defined.
Modular	The Virtual Organisation is built from several organizations which are offering a set of services or resources. These services are provided according to the agreed contracts to the Virtual Organisation, but control and management is *not* delegated to a central instance.

Property	Definition
Heterogeneous	The resource and services by the different participants are not homogeneous. Each member has its strengths and distinct profile and as outlined above may provide even a unique resource.
Dispersed	The members of a VO may be located at different places and also the duration of membership is determined and independent from the membership of others.
Connected	In order to enable a communication between services and resources across organisational boundaries not only technological but to the same extend also procedural or administrative barriers need to be overcome. As simple examples the configuration of firewalls or the dynamic creation of user accounts can be mentioned.
Complex	The management and organisation of services and resources within an organization is already a complex and challenging task. In the geographically and legally dispersed case the problems to be solved are even more complex as a decentralized control is assumed.
Unpredictable	An inherent property of complex systems is the lack of predictability. The relations between the different elements are not fixed and even the VO members, the service providers, may change their structure, resources and services landscape over time which makes also the behaviour unpredictable. As a counter measure the delegation of the management problem to the resource owners and the formal description of the relations between the providers in the form of Service Level Agreement is reducing the probability of unexpected behaviour but is not a guarantee. As described above service provider might even decide to act unreliable in one Virtual Organisation to safeguard a contract in another VO.
Interdependent	A Virtual Organisation is not a linear system and the change of the state and the behaviour might have impact on the state and behaviour of other members in the VO. This property is very closely related to the one above.

2.3 A proposed more sophisticated VO Model

Property	Definition
Bound	As shown in figure 2.1 the boundary of a Virtual Organisation is logically lying *within* an organisation. Furthermore the boundary is different for different Virtual Organisations a service provider is participating.

Table 2.1: Structural properties of Virtual Organisations

2.3.1.1 Topologies

The following sections will outline in more detail potential topologies for Virtual Organisations. They are based on the classification developed by Lethbridge in [9]. Due to the hierarchical nature of Virtual Organisations where a particular service provided to a VO *A* can be either provided by any kind of legal organisation or another Virtual Organisation *B* all presented topologies in the next sections can be combined and used together. For example within a Virtual Organisation that is organised according to the Hub-and-Spoke topology around a main contractor as it is typical for the design of complex products in the automotive or aerospace domain some of the services could be provided instead of a legal organisation by another Virtual Organisation that is organised in Peer-To-Peer topology as shown in figure 2.3. While in the figures 2.2, 2.3, 2.4 a dedicated *consumer* as a specific role is shown in an Business to Business (B2B) scenario this role would be covered by a service provider.

Hub-and-Spoke (Main contractor) The topology of this model is grouped around a core organisation or main contractor that acts as the interface towards the consumer. Several other organisations contribute with services an resources to the objectives of the Virtual Organisation. The Core Organisation is exchanging information with all the services of these organisations. Furthermore the core organisation is expected to coordinate the information flows between the members. Despite the management must suit each member in the Virtual Organisation the overall management is under control of the core organisation.

Example 2.1 *A plane manufacturer is outsourcing part of his business to external organisations such as optimisation of a turbine to a provider of high performance computing services. The process stays under the control of the manufacturer which is also delivering the end product to the consumer.*

Chapter 2 A new Taxonomy for Virtual Organisations

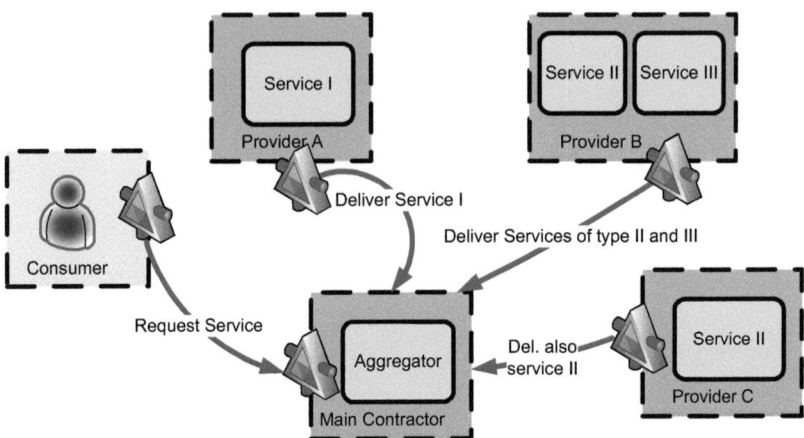

Figure 2.2: Topology for Hub-and-Spoke and Broker scenarios

Broker This is a variation of the previous topology. In this setting again several organisation are placed around a central interface towards the consumer. In contrast to the previous model this central organisation is not acting as the core organisation that cannot be replaced but is simply acting as a central interface toward the customer but is not acting as a single responsible entity and is not controlling the other members in the Virtual Organisation.

Flat Full Hierarchy (Peer to Peer) In this case independent organisations are grouped together with no clear core member. The roles of the organisation can be different and one role could be to build the interface to the consumer but no central controlling entity is present.

Example 2.2 *A possible scenario for this topology is the sharing of data storage capacity across several participants within a Virtual Organisations similar to the widely used file sharing applications.*

Supply Chain (Process oriented) The supply chain or value alliance is structured that each member is using the output of the previous member as input and produce a derived output. The process is started with initial input from the consumer and is ended with the delivery of the final outputs to the consumer. The process might be expressed by a Directed Acyclic Graph (DAG). In this case rather simple process descriptions would be possible. However this topology covers also different kinds of workflow driven interactions using one of the large number of different workflow or choreography languages such as Business Process Execution Language (BPEL) [44], Web

2.3 A proposed more sophisticated VO Model

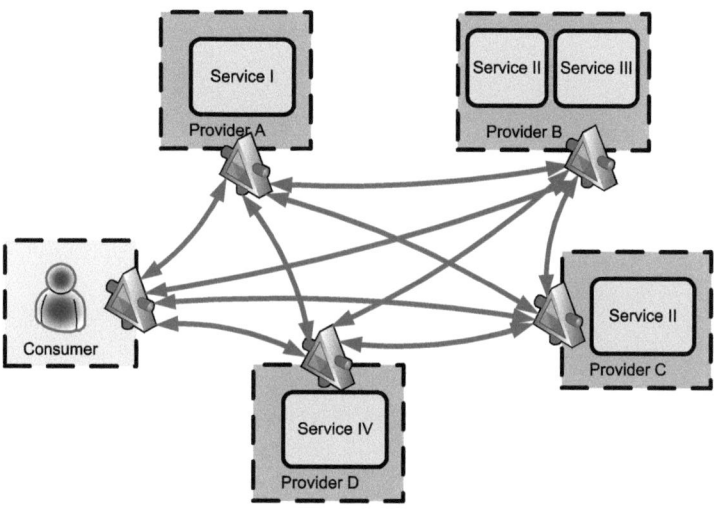

Figure 2.3: Topology for the peer to peer structure

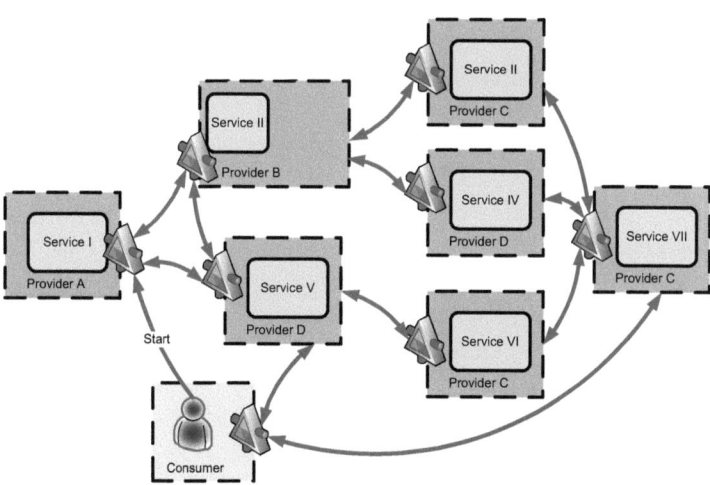

Figure 2.4: Sample topology for the chained structure

Service Choreography Definition Language (WS-CDL) [45] to name a few. Recent developments introduce several layers of process definitions described in a more abstract fashion relying on semantic descriptions that can be mapped to the above mentioned more infrastructure oriented workflow descriptions.

Example 2.3 *A wide range of Grid solutions are organized according to this topology. Early Grid solutions such as Uniform Access over the Internet to Computing Resources [2, 15, 39] where the workflow was described as an acyclic graph called the Abstract Job Object (AJO) built the starting point. Now complex solutions including semantic workflow descriptions exist.*

2.3.2 Role Model

Early definitions of Virtual Organisation assume either that the collaborators are of equal nature (e.g. provider of computational services) or that the roles are limited to service provider and service consumer. Considering a more dynamic model as outlined above with contributors from different companies with conflicting interests new roles that mediate between these stakeholders are needed. Additional supporting the lifecycle of VOs requires new roles. Another aspect is that the number of provided services have been increased from an originally low number (e.g. computing cycle and data storage provider) to more complex service Grids.

In [35] roles in collaborating businesses are defined with a sole economic viewpoint. One of the identified roles is the *broker* acting as the intermediary between the customer and the provider of a service. Additional tasks associated with this role are ranging from marketing up to acquisition and negotiation of new contracts. Beside there is also the role of the *competence manager* delivering the engineering knowledge on available technologies and competencies for the service provider. In this economic model it acts as a supporting role for the broker. Another role is the *project manager* that supervises the Virtual Organisation and is triggering potentially a re-engineering process e.g. by replacing partners that do not perform satisfactorily. The role of the *in and outsourcing manager* is to develop dedicated interfaces for each partner in the Virtual Organisation and offer the technological know-how for the delivery of appropriate and effective services. Furthermore the role of the *auditor* is defined acting as a neutral financial auditor for example in the role of a clearing house. These roles also include the tasks of keeping track of all transactions taken (a kind of provenance service). Aside of this enactment oriented roles Katzy defines also the role of a *network[1]-coach* that acts as a kind of consultancy office for all members of the collaboration. According to Katzy in [35]

---
[1] In [35] network is used similarly to the term Virtual Organisation as used here

...this coaching is necessary to create the indispensable co-operative culture of the network and can be achieved by governance of the network, setting business rules and routines for co-operation, providing technological infrastructures in the network and managing relationships (and conflicts)...

The above mentioned roles are considered to be fulfilled by humans. For the long lived Virtual Organisations considered in the above mentioned paper this is an appropriate solution. However this does not fit the model of the self-organizing Virtual Organisations where for example the reaction time for replacing an underperforming partner might be too short to base it on approval by a human person. This kind of decision must be delegated to a VO management system that is entitled to trigger necessary actions for example based on human defined policies or rules.

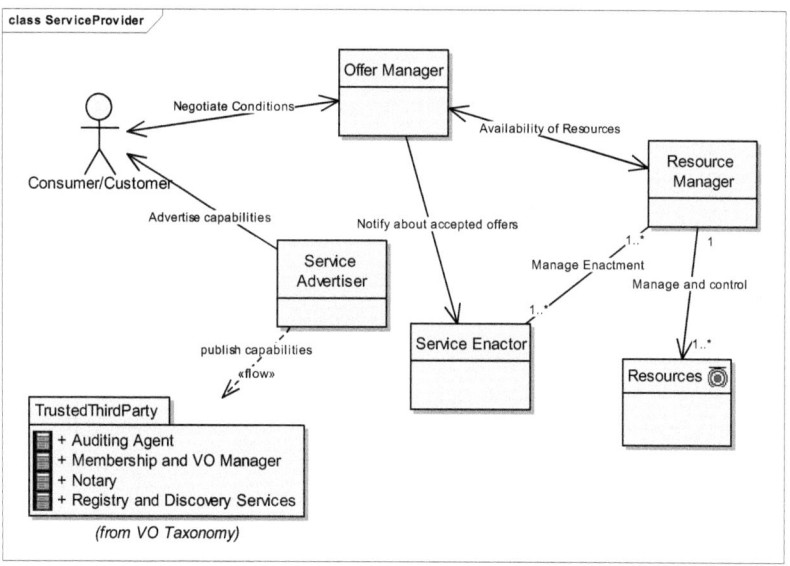

Figure 2.5: Coarse grained view on the roles and their relations in the service provider domain

2.3.2.1 Dynamic Virtual Organisation Roles

In this section the roles in and its interrelations from [35] had been adapted to a more dynamic model assuming the enactment of the roles to be driven by software components only externally configured by humans but not performed by humans. As part of the adaptation, some of the roles had been mapped to several components as the tasks performed by a specific role had been split across the three identified domains, the user domain, the service provider domain and the trusted third party domain. The user domain summarizes the roles and responsibilities performed by the user or more precisely a user agent which is the representation of a user in the system that is configured by the user for example by configuration files, policies or also a user profile that expresses preferences to certain providers which might be based on personal or contract based reasoning. The service provider domain lists all the roles seen for service providers. Often the actors of service providers may either interact directly with the user domain actors or the interaction is done via actors from the trusted third party domain.

2.3.2.2 Service Provider Domain

The service provider domain is characterized best as the entity that has as major purpose the delivery of one or more services to other service providers or the end user. The assumption taken here is that the provision of these kind of services is not done in best effort but requires a decent level of management of the service delivery towards the consumer and that the service level has been agreed in the form of an bilateral Service Level Agreement (SLA). This SLA does not only cover the agreed metrics that allow to measure the quality of the provided services but also lists potential penalties that would be applied in the case of failing to deliver.

Service Advertiser One essential element of a service provider is its capability to advertise the offered services to potential customers. This can be seen as an adaptation of the in/outsourcing manager roles outlined above. The key issue here is that the service must be described detailed enough to allow an automated discovery and integration of the service. In the area of Web Services several standards for this purpose do exist such as Web Service Description Language (WSDL) [46] for describing the functional parameters. Developments such as Semantic Markup for Web Services (OWL-S) [47] can be used to further extend the description beyond functional parameters to a more semantically enriched description.

It is assumed that such descriptions are produced by a human. This person is acting similar to the definition above as the in/outsourcing manager. In order to allow potential consumers of services to query for the service it must be stored in some kind of registries. This role need to be split between a Trusted Third Party (TTP) service that stores static or information that is changing with a low frequency and a local service called Offer Manager that is entitled to negotiate with potential consumers detailed parameters of the service that are individual and/or of dynamic nature.

2.3 A proposed more sophisticated VO Model

So in summary the tasks of the Service Advertiser are to register, de-register and update the static or semi-static information of a services offered by a service provider in Virtual Organisation wide accessible registries.

Offer Manager The Offer Manager acts as the interface to the potential consumer of a service. Upon discovery of a service provider that may offer a service such as delivery of a computational service for a given commercial application with the required machine architecture and type the consumer has decided to start the process of agreeing on a Service Level with the provider in order to safely use the service. The Offer Manager needs to interact with the Resource Manager to understand its current resource availability, with the Service Enactor what other contract had been agreed.

Several kind of negotiation protocols between the consumer and the provider are under research ranging from free negotiation to fixed offers. An intermediary solution is the so called discrete offer protocol ([48]). The discrete offer protocol assumes that different consumers do require different service levels (also driven by the assumption that better service level are more expensive) but a free negotiation is not beneficial as this would make the offers of different service providers not comparable and as also outlined in chapter 5 makes the management a much too complex if not impossible problem. So potentially a service provider might offer a gold, silver, bronze like predefined service level. However this offer might not be possible to be enacted at all time so the task of the offer manager is to understand if the current resource situation allows to offer a certain level such as the silver service or in other words of the risk associated with the delivery of the service versus the potential gain and penalty is balanced. Beside this rather fixed approach more flexible solutions are currently under research as outlined in [49, 50, 51].

Service Enactor Upon acceptance of an offer from consumer and provider side the agreed service need to be provided. The assumption is that it is not sufficient to simply book an appropriate resource and that the enactment of the service does need further interaction. So the first step on acceptance of the offer is to establish an initial set of resources based on the analysis done in the negotiation or planning phase. This start configuration covers all kind of resources ranging from hardware, such as a computational resource, network and software resources to other resources such as licenses.

While this start configuration might be sufficient to guarantee the promised service level in the beginning due to changing conditions e.g. in system or network load or other competing services changes may be necessary. So a Service Enactor need to be able to monitor all involved resources, consolidate them to an overall system status and derive the appropriate measure to be applied in order to react on changing conditions. A typical approach would be that the Service Enactor is driven by external rules or policies.

An important aspect here is that the reaction on changing conditions cannot be limited to one single provided service but that a Service Enactor needs a global view on all currently provided services and potentially needs to prioritise the measures also based on economic considerations such as importance of the customer or associated risk with failure for example based on the agreed critical penalty.

2.3.2.3 User Domain

Within the user domain a set of service supporting the consumer to use the provided facilities either from the Service Provider domain or Trusted Third Party domain are necessary. The listed roles below are the ones that are additionally necessary to integrate with a Virtual Organisation and need to be integrated with other elements e.g. local policy provider or identity and authorization provider. The functionality described here for the User Domain must not necessarily be deployed on a computing system of the End-User but might be delegated to an User Agent acting on the users behalf for this task. In particular as in many deployments the end-users are connected via specific application interfaces or portals the delegation of these tasks is likely to be even the common case.

Service Discovery Interface As outlined above the initial step for establishing an interaction between a consumer and a service provider is the discovery of an appropriate provider. A consumer side component that maps the potentially rather abstract requirements together with local policies is needed that communicate with service registries or service marketplaces to find potential candidates and apply some local policy driven ranking on them. Part of this component can also be interactions with other local services such as authorization components if e.g. the requesting user is allowed to issue external provider requests.

Offer Requestor Based on a list of potential providers a concrete agreement needs to be established with the provider. As the agreement to such an electronic contract requires a defined protocol and content of the exchanged messages to ensure also the legal viability of the agreed contract, a specific component communicating the service quality needs in the required way is essential on the consumer side.

2.3 A proposed more sophisticated VO Model

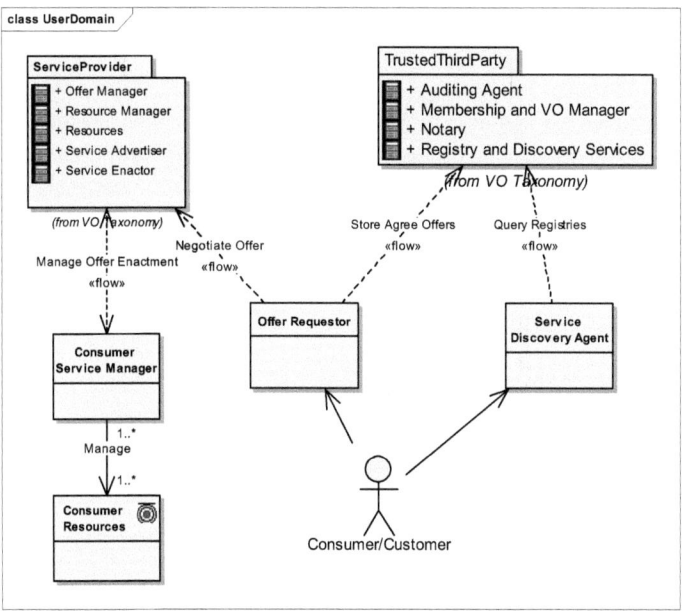

Figure 2.6: Coarse grained view in role interactions from the User Domain viewpoint

Chapter 2 A new Taxonomy for Virtual Organisations

Consumer Service Manager   The agreed contract might impose also restrictions on the consumer side. As an example consider an Service Level Agreement (SLA) that guarantees a maximum response time for a service in case less than 1000 requests per minute are issued. A local management on the user side that makes sure that in case of an increasing need of transactions beyond 1000 requests per minute a new contract is negotiated or an additional service provider is added is necessary in order not to request more than previously agreed. Of course the same applies for an decreasing demand including a full dissolution of the relation.

2.3.2.4 Trusted Third Party

Beside roles that directly contribute to the goals of the Virtual Organisation additional functionality that helps to build, maintain and operate the Virtual Organisation are necessary. While these functions could be delivered in theory by each of the collaborators the establishment of a special role as an intermediary allows "anonymous" communication between Virtual Organisation members and ensure neutrality for services that are supposed to supervise interaction and act as clearing house in case of conflicts. A similar concept has been developed within the TrustCoM project [52] and limited to realising provenance in the Provenance project [53].

Membership and VO Manager   Under the assumption that the provided services cannot be delivered by one single service provider but need to be composed from more basic services delivered by different providers there is a need to locate the potential providers. A selection procedure and the establishment of agreements need to be fostered and supported. This goes far beyond the broker role mentioned above as the interface is not only to one single provider but to a set of orchestrated providers that jointly deliver a complex product or service. An additional aspect is that decisions taken about the set of service providers needs to be communicated or require certain actions such as the subscription to certain event types.

Registry and Discovery Services   The key element of every service oriented architecture is the ability to discover and locate appropriate services. A wide range of approaches do exist. A wide range of approaches exist from simple approaches based solely on functional parameters up to semantic search facilities or market places considering more complex matching scenarios. This service needs to be provided by a Trusted Third Party as neutrality is needed not to give preference to certain providers compared to others in the delivery of matching providers.

2.3 A proposed more sophisticated VO Model

Notary Agreements across organisational boundaries such as Service Level Agreements or any other kind of action that might be a potential source of conflict should be stored in a reliable way by a trusted party.

Auditing Beside the more passive storage and query capability of a notary and active auditing of interactions is necessary. For example in [52] a component called SLAPerformanceLog keeping track of the performance of consumer and provider related to an SLA is foreseen. Similar mechanisms such as performance or responsiveness of partners might be subject to auditing.

2.3.3 Dynamic Viewpoint

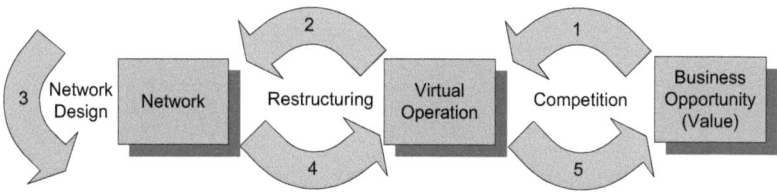

Figure 2.7: Conceptual model and design and implementation of virtual organisation according to Katzy in [11]

In [11] Katzy proposes a conceptual model for the design and implementation of virtual organisations and identifies 5 major change processes describing the evolution of it. The basic assumptions are that the process is driven by a market demand or business opportunity[2] to create a Virtual Organisation and put into operation. Another fundamental assumption is that the organisation is not built from scratch without considering existing business relationships but that the selection of candidates for designing and structuring the operational Virtual Organisation is based on existing business relationships called Enterprise Network (EN). Changes in this Enterprise Network (e.g. a business relationship is ended due to bad performance) also lead to a restructuring process of the Virtual Organisation. Despite the process is driven by an identified business opportunity he claims that the increased agility to react and adopt will also open new markets and therefore create business opportunities. The conceptual model of Katzy is visualized in figure 2.7.

---
[2] referred as "value" in the paper

Chapter 2 A new Taxonomy for Virtual Organisations

Based on this high level model, Saabeel et. al. proposed in [36] an extension to this model. From the 'universe of modules[3]' that would constitute the indefinite set of potential services and modules available the Enterprise Network is built as a small subset of this universe whereas a significantly reduced number of potential service and resource providers are integrated. These providers have agreed on a common set of policies and metadata to describe their services and how they are operated. Out of this Enterprise Network driven by a market demand a Virtual Organisation is built as a combination of services and resources provided by the Enterprise Network. The membership in the Enterprise Network and in the Virtual Organisation are non permanent.

These models are complemented by a lifecycle model developed in the VOMap Roadmap project [54] and in [7, 55]. According to this sources the life cycle of a Virtual Organisation is defined by four phases namely identification, formation, operation and termination. Each of the phases has its distinctive purpose and tasks which are summarised in table 2.2.

Phase	Description
Identification	In this phase the opportunity is discovered that a Virtual Organisation should be formed.
Formation	In this phase the necessary partners are identified and selected. All necessary information is distributed in order to allow all partners act according to the foreseen role.
Operation	In this phase the VO is operational and is aiming to achieve its objectives. During this phase according to the process model outlined above changes to the membership might be necessary to adapt to changing conditions and needs.
Termination	In case the objectives of the VO have been reached the termination phase ends. Typical tasks in this phase are accounting & billing or asset dispersal.

Table 2.2: Lifecycle of a Virtual Organisation

Based on the models and concepts presented above a more sophisticated model for the dynamic viewpoint of Virtual Organisations is presented here. These presented model here is based on the models defined in the frame of several European research projects and published by the author and others in [18, 21, 28].

---
[3]According to the definition provided in table 2.1 this would be services or resources

2.3.3.1 Identification

The identification phase is dealing with setting up the Virtual Organization – this includes selection of potential business partners from the network of enterprises, by using search engines or looking up registries. Generally, identification relevant information contain service descriptions, security grades, trust & reputation ratings or similar information. Depending on the resource types, the search process may consist in a simple matching (e.g. in the case of computational resources, processor type, available memory and respective data may be considered search parameters with clear cut matches) or in a more complex process, which involves adaptive, context-sensitive parameters. For an example, the availability of a simulation program may be restricted to specific user groups or only for certain data types, like less confidential data etc. The process may also involve metadata like security policies or SLA templates with ranges of possible values and/or dependencies between them, such as bandwidth depending on the applied encryption algorithm. The identification phase ends with a list of candidates that potentially could perform the roles needed for the current VO.

After this initial step from the potentially large list of candidates the most suitable ones are selected and turned into VO members, depending on additional aspects that may further reduce the set of candidates. Such additional aspects cover negotiation of actual Quality of Service (QoS) parameters, availability of the service, *willingness* of the candidate to participate etc. It should be noted that though an exhaustive list of candidates may have been gathered during the identification phase, this does not necessarily mean that a VO can be realized - consider the case where a service provider may not be able to keep the promised SLA *at a specific date* due to other obligations.

In principle, the intended formation may fail due to at least two reasons: (a) no provider (or not enough providers) is able to fulfil all given requirements comes to SLA, security etc. or (b) providers are not (fully) available at the specified time. In order to circumvent these problems, either the requirements may be reduced ('choose the best available') or the actual formation may be delayed to be re-launched at a more suitable time. Obviously there may be the case, where a general restructuring of the requirements led to a repetition of the identification phase.

2.3.3.2 Formation

At the end of the (successful) identification phase the initial set of candidates will have been reduced to a set of VO members. In order to allow these members to perform in accordance with their anticipated role in the VO they need to be configured appropriately. During the formation

Chapter 2 A new Taxonomy for Virtual Organisations

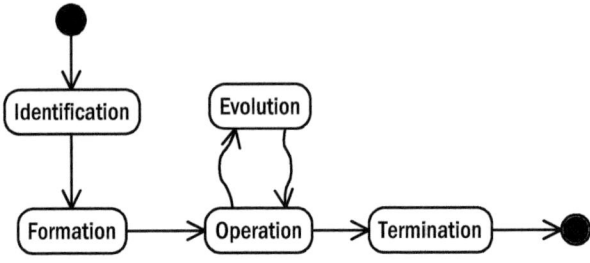

Figure 2.8: Proposed Lifecycle Model for Dynamic Virtual Organisations

phase a central component such as the VO Manager distributes the VO level configuration information, such as policies, SLAs etc. to all identified members. These VO level policies need to be mapped on local policies. This might include changes in the security settings (e.g. open access through a firewall for certain IP addresses, create users on machines on the fly etc.) to allow secure communication or simply translation of XML documents expressing SLAs or Obligations to a product specific format used internally.

After the formation phase the VO can be considered to be ready to enter the operation phase where the identified and properly configured VO members perform according to their role.

2.3.3.3 Operation

The operational phase could be considered the main lifecycle phase of a Virtual Organization. During this phase the identified services and resources contribute to the actual execution of the VOs task(s) by executing pre-defined business processes (e.g. a workflow of simulation processes and pre- and post-processing steps). A lot of additional issues related to management and supervision are involved in this phase in order to ensure smooth operation of the actual task(s). Such issues cover carrying out financial arrangements (accounting, metering), recording of and reacting to participants' performance, updating and changing roles and therefore access rights of participants according to the current status of the executed workflow etc. In certain environments persistent information of all operations performed may be required to allow for later examination e.g. to identify fault-sources (for example, related to the scenario provided below, in case of a plane crash).

2.3.3.4 Evolution

Evolution is actually part of the operational phase: as participants in every distributed application may fail completely or behave inappropriately, the need arises to dynamically change the VO structure and replace such partners. This involves identifying new, alternative business partner(s) and service(s), as well as re-negotiating terms and providing configuration information as during identification, respectively formation phase. Obviously one of the main problems involved with evolution consists in re-configuring the existing VO structure so as to seamlessly integrate the new partner, possibly even unnoticed by other participants. Ideally, one would like the new service to take over the replaced partners task at the point of its leaving without interruption and without having to reset the state of operation. There may other reasons for participants joining or leaving the VO, mostly related to the overall business process, which might require specific services only for a limited period of time - since it is not sensible to provide an unused, yet particularly configured service to the VO for its whole lifetime, the partner may request to enter or leave the VO when not needed.

2.3.3.5 Termination

During termination, the VO structure is dissolved and final operations are performed to annul all contractual binding of the partners. This involves the billing process for used services and an assessment of the respective participants' (or more specifically their resources) performances, like amount of SLA violations and the like. The latter may be of particular interest for further interactions respectively for other potential customers. Additionally it is required to revoke all security tokens, access rights etc. in order to avoid that a participant may (mis-)use its particular privileges. Generally the inverse actions of the formation phase have to be performed during Termination. Obviously partial termination operations are performed during evolution steps of the VO's operation phase (cf. above).

Chapter 3

Classification of Scenarios and Derived Requirements

The requirements derived here are based on the abstraction of requirements from a wide range of scenarios and research projects. The information basis analysed are the application scenarios of the GeneSyS and GRASP projects and the Integrated Projects TrustCoM, NextGrid, Akogrimo and the 18 application scenarios from the largest European research project in the 6th framework programme BEinGRID. These scenarios cover a very wide range of different application sectors.

3.1 The Method for the Scenario Classification

The goal of the thesis to deliver a framework that goes beyond supporting a specific application scenario and provide a more generic solution requires an intermediate step in the requirements analysis. Instead of collecting the requirements for a concrete scenario directly an abstraction and classification process has been necessary to derive a set of typical cases. These cases are then analysed in order to derive the requirements for the framework. Consequently the cases do not represent a full scenario e.g. in its topology but represent a key element that can be found in many of the analysed industrially relevant scenarios.

The pre-conditions for selecting a scenario to be included in the analysis had been that the taxonomy for Virtual Organisations introduced in chapter 2 can be applied to the scenario and that in particular the services are provided across organisational boundaries. As the VO definition is not limited to Grid computational infrastructure scenarios also non-Grid distributed application has been included. Having a broader basis including also more Peer-to-Peer Computing based applications broadens the scope as many Grid scenarios tend to operate in a comparably controlled environment as shown by the author in [56]. Furthermore the classification criteria as defined by

Chapter 3 Classification of Scenarios and Derived Requirements

the author and others in [57] in particular for conglomeration type, hierarchy and management structure had been very useful to perform the abstraction process.

The results of the analysis are documented following the structure below:

1. Short outline of the specific criteria of the scenario
2. Description of the typical processes performed in the phases identification, formation, operation and termination according to the definition in section 2.3.3, in particular in table 2.2 on pages 23 – 24
3. Structure or Topology and communication model based on the definitions in the last chapter in section 2.3.1.1
4. Organisational Structure with a specific focus on the management aspect
5. Identified challenges for the management of this scenario
6. List potential benefits for the scenario if a management framework would be in place and list initial ideas on what kind of components could be useful

3.2 Core Service Provider Scenario

The simplest possible VO consists out of two participants. In this scenario type the additional constraint is that only one participant acts in the provider role for one or more consumers and that the provided service is a core service that directly maps to a physical resource. If the provided service is the delivery of a document potentially generated from a database or Content Management System (CMS) the scenario is a typical web application provider case. But if the services provided are a job submission and monitoring interface to a queuing system of a cluster or a store and retrieve services e.g. for parallel data streams it goes far beyond the simple web application case.

The scenario is very much in line with the so called High Performance Computing (HPC) Basic Profile [58] currently defined within the Open Grid Service Architecture (OGSA) working group of OGF (Open Grid Forum). In this scenario specific extensions to existing standards such as the Job Service Description Language (JSDL) [59] have been defined and put in combination with a simple Execution Management Service called OGSA-BES (Basic Execution Service) [60] . The profile foresees that a task expressed as a JSDL document is submitted to the service provider. The JSDL document is analysed by the BES and transformed to a job in a queuing system. The originator of the JSDL document receives as a reply a confirmation of the successful submission and a jobId to be used for further communication. With this jobId the status of the job can be

3.2 Core Service Provider Scenario

queried (e.g. queued, running, completed, ...), intermediate or final results can be queried or jobs can be cancelled.

As outlined in section 2.3.2 more services on the provider side and on the consumer side are necessary. Additionally to the functionality defined in the HPC Profile before the job can be submitted a Service Level Agreement (SLA) needs to be negotiated and agreed and beside a basic resource scheduling as done by the BES service a more complex selection procedure based beside pure functional also based on economic or organisational rules and policies need to be followed. Additionally several decision points (e.g. security policy driven) are in between the external submission interface and the virtualized resources. In figure 3.1 examples for the building blocks of a Core Service Provider are shown.

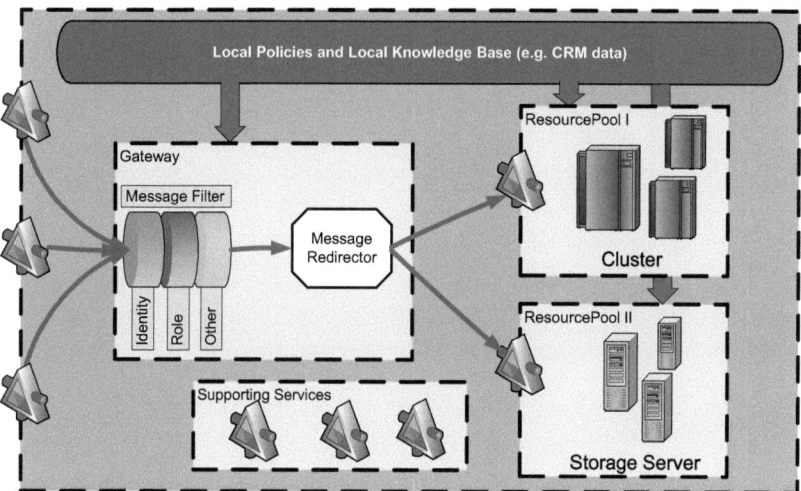

Figure 3.1: Sample Building Blocks of the Core Service Provider Scenario

3.2.1 Topological View

Obviously the topology of the VO is very easy and consists out of one or more consumers potentially from different institutions and one service provider that may have internally a complex chain-oriented infrastructure to deliver the service. In figure 3.2 this topology together with some sample service components is shown.

Chapter 3 Classification of Scenarios and Derived Requirements

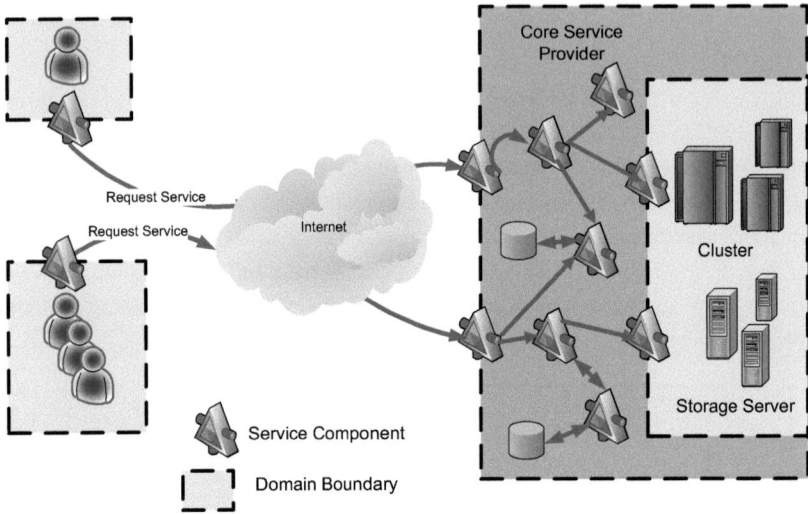

Figure 3.2: Topological View on the Core Service Provider Scenario

In figure 3.2 it is worth to note that components for the management (shown as 'service components') are not only located in the service provider but also on the user domain. Beside the indicated management of the resources and the service components the full range from network, system, network up to the management are part of this topology.

3.2.2 Dynamic View

The following table analysis the specific tasks that might be subject to management along the different lifecycle phases even if some of them are not relevant for this simple scenario.

Phase	Description
Identification	In this scenario the whole service is provided by one single service provider so no partner selection or discovery processes is performed.

3.2 Core Service Provider Scenario

Phase	Description
Formation	As there is no Business to Business (B2B) collaboration between Service Providers is foreseen no dynamic establishment of a business relationship is performed. This also means that no configuration e.g. of opening certain firewall ports to the other provider or set-up and usage of users and groups for controlling access for the collaboration partner is needed. The dynamic aspect is reduced to the consumer part. Depending on the scenarios this might be also a static or semi-static collaboration where a consumer must be pre-determined and published to the provider (personal details, IP addresses of client machines, certificates, ...) or as typical in a portal based approach this process is moved out of the VO by assuming the portal to be the VO participant acting as a User Agent.
Operation	The Operation phase does not impose any specific challenges on the VO level as outlined above no dynamic relationship is targeted. In case of SLA violations or delivery failure no alternative providers are available, so no actions but termination can be performed. Within the service provider domain depending on the internal structure appropriate management of all internal building blocks and the SLA provision need to be enacted.
Termination	Similar to the formation phase this phase is not relevant for this simple scenario.

Table 3.1: Dynamic View for the Core Service Provider Scenario

3.2.3 Key Requirements summary

Although this configuration is rather simple it already delivers an initial set of requirements on a management infrastructure to support this setting.

Req. 1 *Consider Dependencies between components* One obvious requirement for a management solution that can be derived is the need for traceability and dependency information between the components. For example if a job cannot successfully placed in the queuing system this might have a wide range of different reasons. As an example the communication between the server receiving the JSDL document and the server hosting the BES service might be broken. Lots of potential sources for this problem can be easily listed. From failure of physical hardware of the JSDL or BES server, the hosting application such as Apache Tomcat, firewall settings, network connections. In order to trace problems down to a root cause the management framework must have the possibility to go down a dependency graph.

Req. 2 *Need for a common information model* As the resources involved in the delivery of a service are of very different nature and monitored with tools from different vendors the data provided cannot be expected to be in a common format. In order to enable a management on basis of the available information a common information model at least within the service provider domain is essential.

Several formats do exist as of today that might be re-used such as Management Information Base (MIB) used within the Simple Network Management Protocol (SNMP) environment or the Component Information Model (CIM).

Req. 3 *Monitor on all levels* Consequently, the resources and components on different levels need to be considered for a management solution. This means that first of all the monitoring cannot be restricted on application level, but need to cover middleware, operating system, network and all other layers involved in the delivery of a service. Most notably the management must be integrated across all these layers and cannot be done independently as the interdependencies as mentioned above could not be traced.

Req. 4 *Definition of normal system conditions* The global definition of a normal system operation condition is impossible. It is only possible to identify for each of the individual components some boundaries but the prediction and analysis of the overall system behaviour is a non trivial task if not impossible. This constitutes the risk that the overall management of the system is not stable and might collapse.

Req. 5 *Consider organisational limits of self-management* Even in this rather simplified scenario it is already obvious that automated system management is in contradiction with security constraints. Assume the case that a system administrator closes a port as she assumes a security attack. A monitoring component of the firewall could detect this, analyse the problem and conclude that the firewall port is closed but should be open to ensure operation and automatically update the firewall setting to open the port again. As a result some management tasks cannot be fully automated and might be escalated in the appropriate way to a human operator for approval or even delegated completely. This requirements is also related to requirement 1.

3.3 Aggregated Service Provider Scenario

Aggregated Service Provision (AgSP) differentiates from the Core Service Provision that the provided service is more complex and is built from a combination of two or more services. The combined services can be a core service (as defined above as a direct virtualization of a physical resource) or another complex service. An example for a complex service could be the provision of a parameter study service. The consumer would provide configuration information such as application to be used, range of parameters, success or stop conditions. The service provider would detect appropriate resources within the Service Provider domain and would execute either consumer or provider defined workflows, execute several application runs, store the intermediate results, run analysis applications on the results and automatically re-run the next bunch of application runs until a success or stop criteria is met. The major difference to the basic core service scenario is that the service offered is of a different level of abstraction and involves several dependant execution steps and decision processes within the service provider domain. Furthermore the utilized core services and with them the physical resources are changing over time and the monitoring must be adapted in real-time with the changes in the execution of the service.

3.3.1 Topological View

From a topological viewpoint outside the service provider domain no difference to the previous scenario is necessary. However the internal structure of the service provider might be much more complex. Beside the key building blocks of the core service scenario additionally components that are able to locally enact workflow, discover and manage the available resource and aim for an optimised usage of them are possible.

3.3.2 Dynamic View

For the Identification and Termination phase there is no difference to the Core Service Provider scenario above. For this reason they have been removed from the table below.

Phase	Description
Formation	Additionally to the steps in the Core Service Provider scenario a set-up of the complex service provisioning chain is needed. This includes the discovery and allocation of the appropriate core services, establishment of a service enactor responsible for the operation and the local management and optimisation of the allocated resources.
Operation	The orchestration of the services to deliver the complex service to the consumer need to be actively managed and is subject of continuous optimization. This includes the supervision of the progress of the service provision and the interaction with management components that provide alerts and events from the underlying infrastructure. Additionally a re-organisation of the full provisioning chain might be necessary or advisable in order e.g. to reduce costs or maintain the externally agreed SLAs.

Table 3.2: Dynamic View for the Aggregated Service Provider Scenarion

3.3.3 Key Requirements summary

Requirements that have been already mentioned before are not listed again but only the additionally needed capabilities are described. In order to refine existing requirements or to refer to previously mentioned requirements the requirement number is used.

Req. 6 *Integration with the Execution Management Building Block* The provision of a core service is of rather static nature. The steps needed are pre-defined, the involved resources are fixed and the service is not evolving over time. An aggregated or complex service such as the parameter study service given as example above involves more than one service and is evolving over time. This means that that management needs to evolve in a similar way and that communication between the management component and the execution environment is needed. The communication is necessary as in contrast to the core service scenario in case of failure of one ore more elements that are orchestrated a recovery by replacing resources is feasible.

Req. 7 *Standardised Interfaces and Information Models* In addition to the requirement 2 expressing the need for a standardised information model the identified need for communication in requirement 6 imposes the need for a standardized communication interface between consumer and provider of management information. As discussed in chapter 4 no such globally accepted standard exists as of now.

Req. 8 *Management of Service Level Agreements* The flexibility gained with the dynamic orchestration of the service also enables a more active management of the delivered service. In particular if services are provided to more than one consumer and Service Level Agreements have been agreed between provider and consumers the provision of them need to be actively managed. This requires a view across all currently active SLAs as the management of the assets of the service provider by reconfiguring an aggregated service from resource A to resource B does have potential impact on the provision of other concurrently provided services.

As already expressed in requirement 1 it is important to understand the dependencies for delivering a certain service. An additional problem introduced with SLAs is the need to enable the consumer[1] of a service to validate its correct enactment. This means that the elements of such an SLA must be expressed in a way that is not tight to the providing infrastructure for three reasons:

1. a service provider would not like to expose *how* certain services are provided as the provider wants to maintain the possibility to dynamically change and adapt its internal provisioning chain as needed.

2. a consumer is not interested about the internal and is not able to validate if certain boundaries (e.g. bandwidth share of a provider internal connection) is really provided. The consumer needs measurable guarantees at the provider boundary. Related to the bandwidth example this means a guaranteed transfer rate of a data stream between provider and consumer.

3. if SLAs contain internal infrastructure details they are either not comparable or require that all service providers must have the same infrastructure to deliver the service. Both preconditions are clearly not realistic assumptions.

While expressing such requirements on a higher, non infrastructure oriented level, clearly makes sense, it introduces a major challenge. A service provider must be able to map down this abstract level agreements to its concrete infrastructure in order to manage its enactment. Closing this gap for a generic environment is still an open research topic and far from being solved. For this work the limitation of scope assumed is that the SLA negotiation is not possible in a free way but that a limited set of pre-defined cases exist such as gold, silver, bronze like quality bundles for typical cases that can be dynamically selected and where this mapping has been done beforehand.

---

[1] or a third party performing this task on the behalf of the consumer

Req. 9 *Consider non-technical parameters* Related to the requirement 8 there is the need to consider non-technical parameters in the re-configuration and management process. In particular if the available resources and assets are reduced e.g. due to failures or overcommitment a decision needs to be taken how to distribute the scarce resources. As in such a situation it is likely that not all SLAs (in the worst case none) can be fulfilled a prioritisation is needed to ensure that at least the most *important* ones are realised. The importance is not defined by technical parameters but could be derived from status of the consumer, the agreed penalty of violating the SLA, the performed task or expected income on successful completion to name a few possibilities. For example if the consumer is an important customer a violation of an SLA might have an impact on the future business relation due to reduced reputation and must be avoided. More general non-technical parameters such as consumer status, business relations, economic considerations but also importance of the executed tasks (e.g. supporting an emergency situation or a treatment of a patient) need to be considered.

3.4 Service Provider Collaboration

The scenarios discussed so far in the previous sections had been limited to one single service provider. The fundamental motivation behind a VO is the collaboration of Service Providers in a Business to Business (B2B) topology. Whereas the above mentioned scenarios are organised merely in a client/server topology here a multi-provider scenario is described. The Service Provider Collaboration case combines the above mentioned scenarios. The VO in this scenario is built from several core and aggregated service providers that might include additionally[2] one or more consumers.

In figure 3.3 a sample setting for a multi-provider scenario from a collaborative engineering case abstracted from the demonstrator of the TrustCoM project is shown. In this example scenario an engineer from an aerospace company wants to design an antenna for the equipment of an airplane with Wireless Local Area Access Network (WLAN) functionality. Beside the access to product design databases that could contain data of the aircraft surfaces, internal structures, avionics etc. the provision of storage services, an application for calculating antenna characteristics and the necessary computational infrastructure is needed. The basic configuration of the VO and a typical workflow is shown in figure 3.3.

---

[2]The consumer role is not essential as one or more providers can act as peers covering the provider and consumer role

3.4 Service Provider Collaboration

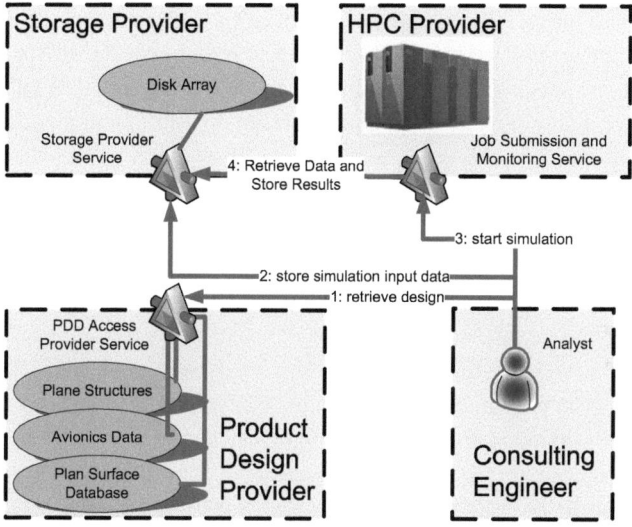

Figure 3.3: The Service Provider view of the Collaborative Engineering Scenario

3.4.1 Topological View

This scenario can be operated in a wide range of different topologies. The simplified view expressed in figure 3.3 assumes an equal role between the three providers and does not limit the communication between the nodes. However a more realistic assumption would be that one of the service providers would act as the entry point for the customer/consumer and potentially even hide that the service is provided relying on 3rd party services.

In many scenarios analysed a main contractor is delivering a complex service to the customer. This service is build from internal and external services delivered by other providers. But the control and management of the subordinary services is performed by this main contractor leading to a hub-and-spoke like topology (refer to section 2.3.1.1 and the sophisticated taxonomy done by the authors and others in [57]). While this setting is the most common one theoretically also a more Peer-to-Peer Computing like interaction model is feasible and also in place in industrial cases. As an example for the more Peer-to-Peer Computing oriented topology one can consider a joint bid of Small and Medium Enterprises in competition with a bigger competitor or for projects with high risks such as the design of a very large airplane.

As in this case in contrast to the single provider scenarios a specialisation of the services provided is possible it is also typical that the different providers fulfil different roles. In the sample scenario the different roles are defined by their contribution of data and resources to the distributed application. Another possibility to split the responsibilities is to assign certain infrastructure services to a dedicated provider such as resource discovery, notary or other generic services. The pre-condition is that this provider is seen as trustworthy from all other participants or is bound by binding contracts to deliver these services in a fair way.

3.4.2 Dynamic View

This case is difficult to generalise from a dynamic viewpoint as several common cases exist. One possible case is that a static collaboration exists between the service providers. This means that a typically small group of providers have agreed to collaboration conditions out of band documented in a paper contract and that the structure of the VO does not change during the whole operation. Other options are Dynamic Collaboration Grids or Ad-Hoc Collaboration Grids ([57]) where providers are dynamically selected from a pool of pre-determined providers or are completely freely selected. The table below considers the Static Collaboration and the Dynamic Collaboration Grids as they are the most commonly deployed solutions and Ad-Hoc collaboration Grids are so far in an purely experimental stage (see for example the analysis done by the author in [56]).

Phase	Description
Identification	In the case of static collaboration this task is limited to a selection from the available well known options. In the more generic dynamic multi service provider scenario the identification of the providers might be a complex and time consuming activity. A wide range of discovery mechanism exist from simple functional matching e.g. using the Universal Directory and Discovery Interface (UDDI) interface up to semantic matching algorithms or virtual market places. Important to note here is the assumed limitation on pre-known providers that are either static or limited from a pool of providers (e.g. called BaseVO or Virtual Breeding Environment (VBE)). This limitation simplifies the case as from all service providers a set of supported functionality (required and optional interfaces) and support of data and policy formats can be assumed.

3.4 Service Provider Collaboration

Phase	Description
	So the steps performed in the identification phase are to reduce the potentially large list of candidates from the pool to a smaller candidate set that *potentially* join the VO. While for the management aspects it is irrelevant how the providers are pre-selected it is important to note that the membership within a VO must be considered as dynamic with changing roles and responsibilities ranging from small changes up to the extreme cases of withdrawal from a running VO or joining into an existing, running VO.
Formation	In order to establish the VO the concrete providers have to be selected from the candidate set of the identification phase. In this phase concrete negotiations with the providers further reduce the candidate set to a list of ranked options and finally a decision on the providers that join initially the VO is taken. For the selected providers a set of configuration information need to be exchanged before the operation phase can start. Part of this process is also the establishment of the monitoring of the service and the local and VO wide management processes. In addition to this VO wide tasks as outlined before for the core and aggregated service provider scenarios a set of provider internal steps need to be performed that are not repeated here again.
Operation	During the operation phase additional steps as outlined for the single provider scenario are necessary. While so far the management could be focused on provider internal activities for this case also a VO wide management is needed.
Evolution	A major potential difference is that a service or whole provider might be replaced during the operation phase moving from operation to the evolution phase. In this phase a service A provided by provider *foo* that is not operating properly (e.g. based on observations of the management system and corresponding SLA violation notifications) is replaced by another service. It could be replaced by service A offered by another provider *bar*, or an internal re-allocation within *foo* could be a solution.

Phase	Description
	This re-allocation might also involve additional recovery steps e.g. moving back in the workflow to the last checkpoint position and corresponding penalty actions on the failing provider up to removing the provider from the VO or reducing its role.
Termination	In case the VO is terminated also all established management activities need to be stopped. Additionally the performance of the providers is analysed.

Table 3.3: Dynamic View for the Multiple Service Provider Scenario

3.4.3 Key Requirements summary

As the multi provider case is seen as a combination of the single provider cases all requirements listed so far do apply as well for this case. In particular requirement 7 is absolutely essential as operating across organisational boundaries. Beside standards based access and communication models also the semantics of the communicated data need to be aligned and understandable to allow a direct comparison between the providers.

Req. 10 *Management need to be hierarchical* Following the line of the more general requirement 9 operating in an environment involving more than one organisation considering economic and commercial boundary conditions the site autonomy needs to be respected. This means that the management needs to be done on several levels. Beside one potential VO wide management level each provider does have one or more management levels within its domain.

The assumption of site autonomy is a clear requirement expressed in many business oriented scenarios. Related to the need of a VO wide management additional to service provider internal management in [56] for the 18 scenarios in BEinGRID an analysis has been performed by the author of this thesis with the result that 61% of the experiments expressed their need in a central management component and that in particular if the type of collaboration is dynamic the distributed management approach (39%) is prefered. The lack of any kind of management on VO level was not part of the experiments (0%).

Req. 11 *Pro-active and adaptive management approaches* As outlined above the services combined in a virtual organisation may change over time. While some changes have only local impact

3.4 Service Provider Collaboration

(e.g. internal re-organisation of service provision) some changes affect the management on VO level and potentially other providers.

Based on this, two related requirements on the management can be derived:

- the provider internal management needs to be pro-active and needs to anticipate problems in the service provision according to agreed boundaries before they actually happen as an internal re-allocation avoid the application of penalties with the bad impact of decreased reputation and potential side affects on the other provided services up to the exclusion from a VO.
- the management solution needs to be enable fast reaction and adaptation to changing conditions. An applied internal or external re-allocation need to be followed by a corresponding change in the management configuration.

Req. 12 *Defined escalation strategy* Assuming a hierarchical management model also raises the question when a detected problem should be solved within a certain level and when an escalation of the problem is needed to resolve it.

As a refinement of requirement 10 above it is necessary to assign to each management level objectives and boundaries for finding local solutions and to define a clear escalation strategy. A typical provider internal policy would be to allow local problem solving but to notify the next level in the hierarchy about the issue and chosen solution strategies. The higher level could overrule and take measures on its level. While this strategy would be feasible across organisational boundaries typically internal problems are not reported to the outside and either treated internally or the provider aims to find external help actively (e.g. outsourcing of functionality to a 3rd party instead of asking a VO wide management body to find a solution.

Req. 13 *Mediated information flow* In the ideal case all available information about the distributed system is used to take the appropriate management decisions. But not all information is supposed to be available to all participants and additionally in larger systems collecting *all* information available is clearly also a scalability issue. The need to filter or translate information is consequently driven by technical and commercial requirements.

From a technical viewpoint the flood of information needs to be reduced and aggregated on several levels from raw information to a more abstract event. This abstraction or translation process also includes a mapping from a proprietary information format to a provider internal standard in order to allow comparability of the collected data. As this abstraction also means the loss of information it might be necessary to query for more detailed information on a case by case basis.

Chapter 3 Classification of Scenarios and Derived Requirements

While the above mentioned reason would apply also for the delivery of fine grained information across organisational boundaries, additionally site autonomy, confidentiality and privacy do not allow the provision of all kind of information. So depending on the role and the access rights associated with this role a subset of information is provided outside the administrative boundaries of a provider.

In case an internal re-allocation of resources is necessary to meet an agreed service quality by moving from a cheap to a more precious resource this is nothing a provider want to communicate outside of the provider domain. Another example is that a provider is willing to guarantee a certain service quality to the consumer (including potentially a dynamically negotiated price), but providing the information about a low load situation would be clearly counter productive in particular if the prize for the service is not fixed. But also in the case of a fixed price the provider would preferably communicate guaranteed start times for a service rather than than low level *internal* information such as the current length of the queues of a cluster system.

Consequently the information flow to external consumers needs to be mediated and controlled.

3.5 Virtual Laboratories

The Virtual Laboratory is a special case of the multi provider case described in the previous section. It summarises scenarios where there is a difference between the designer of the distributed application and the actual user of the pre-configured distributed application. The motivation to name this kind of setting a virtual laboratory is inspired by the projects *A virtual laboratory for decision support in viral diseases treatment (VIROLAB)* [61] and *Virtual Laboratory for eScience (VL-E)* [62] projects that introduced this name. But also in a couple of other projects in particular in the domain of semantic Grids the concept of splitting the design and execution of a distributed application within a Virtual Organisation is rather common. A sample of this type is the *Knowledge based Worflow Systems for Grid Applications (K-Wf Grid)* project [63] .

The difference to the multi provider scenario is mostly in the dynamic view where the application design (decoupling of design and execution) and also the knowledge conservation in the termination phase is taken as an additional step beyond the already described wrap-up tasks. From a topological viewpoint the difference is in the need of several user roles.

3.5.1 Topological View

As the Virtual Laboratory is essentially a multi provider scenario no significant difference in the topology can be expected. As mentioned above the major difference lies in the introduction of several user roles. In VIROLAB [61, 64] these roles are named *Experiment developer*, *Experiment user* and *Clinical Virologist*. The designer plans, designs and implements the scientific experiments conducted on the Grid infrastructure. The experiment user benefit from this pre-defined experiments by providing the necessary input data and parameters to execute them and to achieve results. As VIROLAB targets for application in the medical domain the data user is a *Clinical Virologist*.

So the difference is that several users potentially situated at different sites are using the overall setting in different roles. The Application Designer performs steps to identify a useful business process[3] and need to attach appropriate meta-data to each individual step allowing an Application User to correctly parametrize the pre-defined process and start it. Additionally there is the role of a data retriever that is working with the results produced be one ore more executed processes.

3.5.2 Dynamic View

Phase	Description
Identification	The list of candidates is additionally reduced by constraints provided by the application designer. The designer could for example limit a certain step to a group of providers or even to a particular provider (e.g. internal). While the data associated to each task is based on concretely available services at design time typically no fixed provider is determined in this phase but only a set of describing parameters.
	Based on this preparatory steps the Application User completes the identification phase with starting the application execution process. Upon identification and potential adaptation of the prepared application the formation phase is entered.
Formation	This phase is rather similar to the steps described in table 3.3. The only difference is that potentially additional constraints in the selection process determined by the Application Designer further decrease the list of candidates.

[3]while in a scientific environment a better name would be experiment this term is assumed to be more general

Phase	Description
Operation	Based on the assumed limitations based on the application design not all potentially available solution strategies might be applicable as they had not been e.g. foreseen for this user role. A typical case is that the meta-data for tasks in the process contain rules such as 'switch only between local services' indicating the solution strategy to relocate to a service only within the service provider domain. With this pre-defined solution strategy the potential approach to relocate the service to an external provider if no appropriate local provider can be found cannot be selected.
Evolution	As outlined above the evolution strategy might be also designed and therefore limited in the way an evolution can be performed.
Termination	An essential part of such environments is that the experience with a designed application is stored. The experience can be collected automatically (e.g. whether the designed problem solving strategies did succeed or fail, time to implement such a change), but can also collect the level of satisfaction of the application user.

Table 3.4: Dynamic View for the Virtual Laboratory Scenario

3.5.3 Key Requirements summary

Req. 14 *Support for externally defined solution strategies* The major additional requirement of this scenario is the need to support externally defined management goals and solution strategies. As part of the application design the Application Designer might define already the appropriate measures to be taken in case of certain failures. This might affect VO level policies which could be for example not to replace an underperforming service provider but to pause or terminate the VO instead.

Additionally one could imagine also that the application design requires the need to communicate all internally used resources, their status and the application of recovery or other management actions as the performed tasks is of high risk. Another (more likely) option could be to limit possible solutions strategies e.g. preventing a service re-allocation to another physical resource.

3.6 Interactive Instrument or Simulator Integration

Beside the issues addressed so far, some scenarios impose further requirements as they integrate large and unique physical equipments or physical simulators into a Virtual Organisation. One example for this class of applications is an interactive simulation for astronauts of the international space station [65] as shown in figure 3.4. How a management approach based on human operators needs to be realised has been analysed by the authors and others in [31, 32, 33, 34].

Another class of applications that are related are addressed in the research projects *Grid Enabled Remote Instrumentation with Distribtued Control and Computation (GridCC)* [66] and *Remote Instrumentation on Next Generation Grids (RinGrid)* [67] . Instead of a physical simulator such as the automated transport module as in the previous example instruments such as radio telescopes are virtualized and integrated. As these special resources are very precious resources the flexibility is significantly reduced.

3.6.1 Topological View

From a topological viewpoint there are one or more services that are seen as wrappers to a large external system or an external interactive simulation that is not following an SOA paradigm and is for example based on the Run-Time-Infrastructure (RTI).

This means that in this scenario not the full topology is known or can be controlled and that special management interfaces are necessary to be exposed directly from the resource or the external distributed simulation.

3.6.2 Dynamic View

As the integration of such an equipment would be an add-on to all scenarios, in particular the virtual laboratory the table below focus on the specific issues around the virtualized equipment and does cover the steps needed to set-up the full VO including *regular* services.

Phase	Description
Identification	As the special resources are either rare or unique no real identification phase can be done for them as the goal to reduce the list of potential candidates has achieved already beforehand.

Phase	Description
Formation	Instead of a negotiation with service provider about the quality of a certain service level it is more the reservation of access. However, based on the scheduled access time the supporting services need be configured and negotiated to support the necessary quality level.
Operation	During the operation phase, the whole management process aims to provide an optimal usage of the precious resource. In case the supporting services cannot fully provide the necessary service level it might be necessary to pause the operation until all conditions are met again and a resume of the application can be performed.

Table 3.5: Dynamic view for scenarios with special or unique resources

3.6.3 Key Requirements summary

In this section the additional requirements originating from this scenario are listed. Previously listed requirements remain also valid for this scenario.

Req. 15 *Provide special attention to essential services* While this requirement is pretty obvious in this case, the assumption that some services are essential or of high priority and need special attention from the management side is true for a more general set of scenarios. It can be assumed that in all Virtual Organisations some services might be optional in the sense that they have a negative impact on the VO results (e.g. delay) in case of underperformance, but do not lead to an overall failure. Essential services lead to a failure of delivery of the VO in case of failure or critical underperformance.

Req. 16 *Interaction with other management systems* In the above mentioned case beside the SOA based distributed application there is another distributed application, the interactive simulation, executed in parallel. Such applications might have already a management system that needs to be integrated.

So it is not enough to see all external entities as pure passive data providers but as potentially active components that react themselves already on changing conditions.

3.7 Context dependent Applications

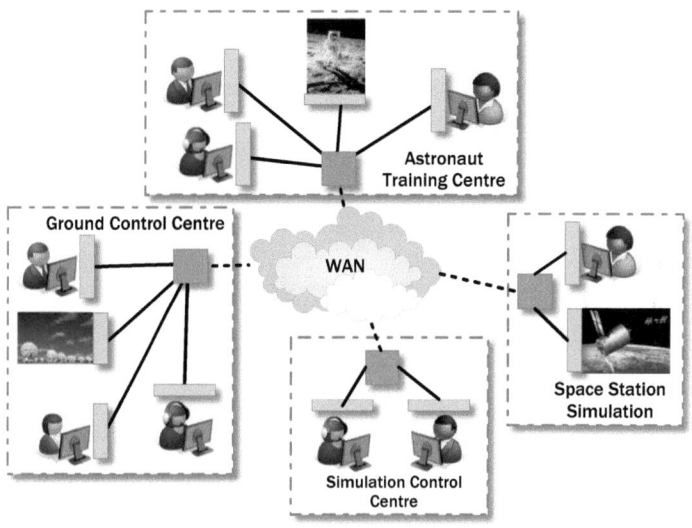

Figure 3.4: Example setting of the space simulation scenario

3.7 Context dependent Applications

Additional requirements originate from a special type of application scenarios as investigated by the author of this thesis in [20]. The assumption taken so far is that the context of the consumer or provider must not be considered. However if the context such as the current network bandwidth or the device capabilities may change over time additional requirements need to be considered such as different type of mobilities [68]:

- **nomadic and mobile users/providers** due to the change of location and consequently the access network the available bandwidth is changing. Furthermore no continuous connectivity can be assumed. This requires the support of an offline mode (a user is temporarily disconnected while the rest of VO remains active) and adaptation to changing network conditions. as an example a user might be connected using an Universal Mobile Communication System (UMTS) connection participating with a low profile. Changing to a Wireless Local Area Access Network (WLAN) Hotspot and a consequently better connection the user can participate with the full profile. Other context parameters might be if the user is in a secure or insecure area affecting the delivery of confidential data.

- **session mobility** the change of a device influence the distributed application as it requires also an adaptation. An example could be the submission of a simulation job from a workstation and the a job monitoring client that provides intermediate results in high quality. Then the user can move the job monitoring client to his mobile phone with a reduced functionality such as a simple percentage of progress or number of completed parameter studies or similar. Later on the job monitor might be moved to a Cave Automatic Virtual Environment (CAVE) environment. Part of this *session* would be that the identity of the user is maintained and the access modalities such as to the data produced is kept unchanged.

3.7.1 Key Requirements summary

Req. 17 *Limit impact of context changes on normal system conditions* As outlined before in requirement 4 the basis for an automated management is the definition of boundaries or goals representing a normal system condition.

Assuming that the context of a consumer or provider can change over time in a similar way the goals/boundaries of the management components need to be adapted. The requirements to adapt the management procedure to a changing context open a wide range of problems. Some of them related to the management of SLAs are discussed by the author and others in [49].

The problem raised in the above mentioned article is that context changes might be quite similar to error conditions. So if a mobile service provider such as a virtualized temperature or health frequency sensor is unavailable it might be that this indicates a problem but could be simply a short disconnection. Such disconnection problems would be clearly and error in the case of an all wired scenario but in this case must be seen as a regular situation. This means that the management solution must be able to differentiate between mobile providers and fixed providers and should adapt the management situation to the context of the provider.

Additionally one could not assume an SLA to be fixed for the lifetime of the Virtual Organisation as if an SLA for a high speed data delivery has been agreed in a high bandwidth context the enactment of the SLA in a changed context of a low bandwidth connection makes obviously no sense.

3.8 Analysis Summary

The presented typical application cases based on the wide range of Grid applications analysed for this thesis indicate that a generic management solution for the type of Virtual Organisations considered here that are spanning organisational boundaries is a distributed solutions itself. One can

3.8 Analysis Summary

say that this is not a surprising result but considering the current practice, typically a centralized approach is used. This central management entity is collecting all the data and performs a centralized management e.g. for the distribution of computational tasks and relies on local management done by humans to make the underlying resources operational. There is no interlinking between this local management and the Grid management layers. Additionally the connecting network is not part of the management solution.

The reason for the currently existing centralized solutions is clearly the reduced complexity compared to a distributed solution. However the key differentiator in the considered scenarios in this chapter is that they are not addressing a pure eScience community, but consider a more economically driven approach. If the decisions to provide a service are driven from optimization goals such as maximise profit and not provide the best service possible one needs to establish a kind of electronic contract, ensuring the collaboration of the providers and one cannot rely anymore on the good will of all participants. So in all scenarios this lack of control is acknowledged and the relationship between providers and between consumer and provider are protected by dynamically or statically established Service Level Agreements. This non-technical but structural constraint imposes a clear boundary between the provider and user domains and the supporting services that enable the collaboration.

From a service provider perspective a couple of externally agreed SLAs for different customers need to be fulfilled. It is irrelevant for the provider internal management for what purpose the provided services are used by the consumers. So the focus of the management approach can be fully on how to meet the Service Level Objectives (SLO) and perform a provider internal optimisation of the resources. This explicitly includes the case where an SLA is intentionally not respected in order to make sure other agreements for a more important customer or associated higher penalty in case of failure can be realised.

From the viewpoint of the management components on Virtual Organisation level they only care about one particular VO and do not consider potentially other competing VOs on this resource. They can rely on the agreed SLAs with the providers and monitor compliance with them. If SLAs are not respected they can trigger the necessary actions on their level e.g. to replace the provider or accept the underperformance and compensate with the agreed penalty.

The approach in the user domain is quite similar to the service provider domain. The management of the consumer side duties must also be managed across several providers, but potentially also across several VOs. An agreed SLA is not only imposing constraints on the provider. For example if a certain number of licenses are granted simultaneously a consumer must make sure that not more then the agreed number are requested. Requests above the agreed threshold would be either rejected or provided at higher costs as they are outside of the original contract.

Chapter 3 Classification of Scenarios and Derived Requirements

With the notion of SLAs between the different roles in the Virtual Organisation the problem of management of quite complex distributed application has been reduced significantly and is brought much closer to current practice in business.

Chapter 4

State of the Art and Relevant Standards

In chapter 2 a new model for Virtual Organizations has been described and how it has been developed from the orthogonal baselines from the world of economics and Grid computing without touching the underlying technologies needed to realise this model. Driven by the scope of the VO model a variety of different distributed application scenarios had been analysed, classified and a set of key requirements has been listed in chapter 3.

In this chapter existing technology and architectures for the management of distributed applications are presented. As a technological baseline a short introduction into the concept of Service Oriented Architecture (SOA) is given. The chapter is concluded with a gap analysis between the requirements identified in chapter 3 and the capabilities of the analysed technologies and concepts in this chapter.

4.1 Core Technologies

One of the fundamental assumptions taken in this thesis to align the solution with the paradigm of Service Oriented Architecture (SOA) based distributed systems as for example defined in [69] and recently adopted also by the Grid community in [24] with the move from proprietary protocols and solutions towards the Open Grid Service Architecture (OGSA). Additionally this section covers existing Grid solutions and their properties and selected Web Service specifications.

4.1.1 Service Oriented Architecture

Service Oriented Architecture (SOA) frameworks are designed to support the dynamic and flexible set-up of applications aggregated as needed from services potentially provided by different

Chapter 4 State of the Art and Relevant Standards

providers from different administrative domains as needed. Service Oriented Architecture is generally seen as the 3rd generation of distributed software component architectures. After the basic Remote Procedure Call (RPC) mechanisms where functions or procedures are made dynamically available and object oriented or object based architectures such as Common Object Request Broker (CORBA) and Distributed Component Object Model (DCOM) now complete components are made available dynamically and the components are only *loosely* coupled. The concept of Service Orientation is actually similar to ideas found in Object Orientation (OO) and Component Based Development (CBD). Services represents natural building blocks combining certain capabilities similar to classes in Object Orientation or components and provide them via a clearly defined interface. The grouping of information and the definition of an interface that hides the complexity and elements inside the service are however chosen on a higher level of abstraction compared to objects.

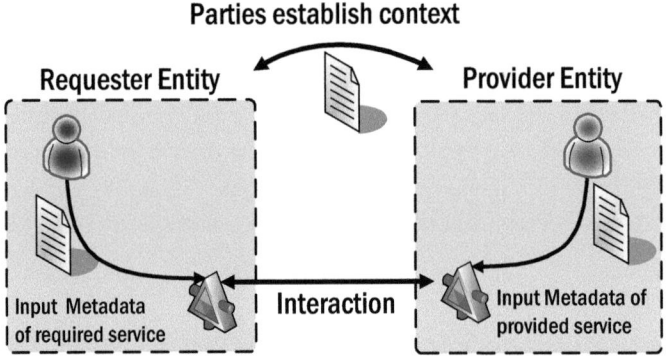

Figure 4.1: Basic concept of the Service Oriented Architecture

Additionally Service Oriented Architecture is targeting *loosely* coupled conglomerations of service providers. All concepts are on a different level of granularity and whereas in Object Orientation the information hiding is about an internal state or mechanism within the object an external service hides company internal procedures, physical resources used to provide the service and represents a virtualization of a potentially highly complex process.

The fundamental characteristics of Service Oriented Architecture include:

- Service providers - publishing the availability of their services.
- Service brokers - registering and categorizing published services and providing search services.

- Service requesters - using broker services to find a needed service and then employing that service.
- Computer-accessible, hierarchical categories, or Ontologies - based upon what the services in each category do and how they can be invoked. These taxonomies aim to assist the dynamic automated discovery of appropriate services.

In order to enable the collaboration among entities within these main roles standardized network protocols and service descriptions are needed. Service descriptions are key to all three roles providing the information needed for an collaboration between the services. In a service-oriented view, the interoperability problem can be broken down into three sub problems: (1) the definition of service interfaces, (2) the identification of the protocol(s) that can be used to invoke a particular interface and (3) a mechanism to negotiate the means of interaction.

Technologies for distributed applications do exist for many years and a partially widely used in industry such as Client-Server [70] and Java 2 Enterprise Edition (J2EE). Other solutions for a more loosely coupled, often asynchronous communication are available with Message Oriented Middleware (MOM) or Peer-to-Peer Computing (P2P).

While Service Oriented Architecture is technology agnostic the most prominent realisation is realised with Web Services [69]. It is globally accepted that Web Services play a key role in the global IT industry (see for example [26, 71, 72]). Peer-to-Peer Computing is also widely accepted especially for data sharing applications.

As the focus of the work is in Business to Business (B2B) interactions of loosely coupled providers the core technologies considered are in line with the Service Oriented Architecture (SOA) paradigm and its Web Service based realisation.

Additionally to the above mentioned property of a different level of granularity in the design of the distributed applications compared to OO applications Web Services have been designed to allow orthogonal and composable specifications. The wide variety of specifications also often referred as *WS-** can be combined in multiple ways. As an example the WS-Addressing [73] specification can be used together with WS-Security [74] but WS-Addressing can be also used together with other specifications.

Further information about Web Services and their application can be found in [75].

4.1.2 Grid computing

As in chapter 6 the application of the framework is evaluated in the context of a High Performance Computing (HPC) service provider also Grid solutions focused to the HPC domain are discussed

Chapter 4 State of the Art and Relevant Standards

here. However the description is not limited to purely HPC oriented Grids but the more general model expressed in OGSA based grids [24, 1] are considered.

The Open Grid Service Architecture (OGSA) [24] leverage the existing Grid frameworks to the level of Service Oriented Architecture (SOA). As outlined above Service Oriented Architecture (SOA) provide the shared organizing principles that underpin the collaborative operation of services in open dynamic distributed systems. The focus is on how services are described and organized to support their dynamic, automated discovery and use at run-time and are not based on manually hard-wired interactions, such as those used in Electronic Data Interchange (EDI) systems.

Originally the OGSA vision was planned to be implemented using the Open Grid Service Infrastructure (OGSI) framework [76]. The key differentiator between OGSI and vanilla Web Services had been the support for stateful service interactions compared to the stateless nature of Web Services. As in the Web Service community also the exposure of state and long term transaction oriented interaction emerged a convergence between these two communities developed. As the OGSI approach would have required significant changes to already well established core web service specifications such as Web Service Description Language (WSDL) [46] the realisation of state a new set of specifications, the Web Service Resource Framework (WS-RF), emerged. These specifications has been standardised by Organization for the Advancement of Structured Information Standards (OASIS). Further competing approaches such as the Representational State Transfer (REST) [77, 78] approach or the less complex related specifications WS-Transfer, WS-Enumeration and WS-Eventing [79] do exist[1].

A large number of research work addresses additions or extensions of this base specifications or middleware solutions. For example the automation of resource discovery and selection or workflow deployment from user level abstract descriptions to an executable environment. Examples include the K-Wf Grid project [63], the Fraunhofer Resource Grid [80] or the ASKALON framework [81].

4.1.2.1 UNICORE

Within the research projects Uniform Access over the Internet to Computing Resources (UNICORE) ([15, 39]) and UNICORE Plus ([2]) a service oriented middleware enabling seamless access to high performance computing resources has been developed. It is mostly a 4-tier architecture consisting of clients, gateway, servers and backend systems.

---

[1]As of now a convergence between WS-RF and the WS-Transfer family of specifications is planned and announced for 2008

4.1 Core Technologies

The jobs defined within Uniform Access over the Internet to Computing Resources are based on a proprietary workflow description called Abstract Job Object (AJO) ([82]) containing not only the involved applications and services of the workflow but also their interdependencies and resources needed. The Uniform Access over the Internet to Computing Resources system is dedicated to the access of High Performance Computing (HPC) resources but aims at the full integration of these resources into a standard e-commerce infrastructure as outlined in [83]. As shown in figure 4.2 a job is passed via a gateway at the service provider to an Network Job Supervisor and is then put further to the Target System Interface after the Abstract Job Object had been mapped using the information in the Incarnation Database to a format understood by the target compute system.

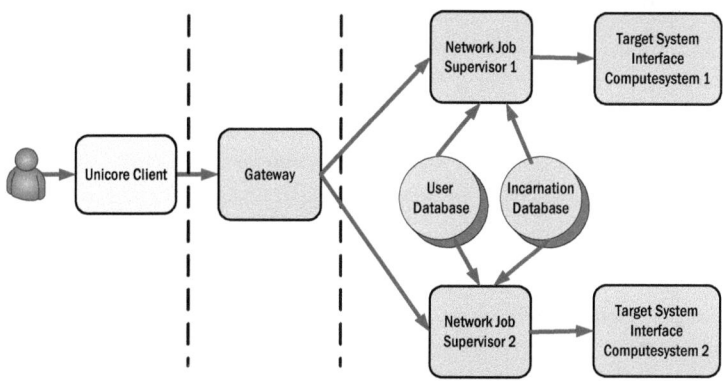

Figure 4.2: UNICORE architecture

Based on this initial work a set of European and national research projects has further developed this infrastructure. Recently the proprietary communication protocols has been replaced by projects like UniGrids [84] or OMII-Europe [85] with standards based communication protocols and interfaces. UNICORE is widely deployed and used in production for example within the Distributed European Infrastructure for Supercomputer Applications (DEISA) project [3].

As UNICORE is not limited only to a middleware but delivers components up to the application support layer and for supporting the service provider management and configuration also an operational model of the virtual organisation is anticipated. A typical UNICORE Virtual Organisation consequently operates in an environment where UNICORE identities are centrally managed but the process of mapping this global identity to a local user is fully under control within each service provider. In general the autonomy of the providers is fully preserved. This rather static approach limits (intentionally) the level of dynamism of the membership in particular for service providers. Currently more complex security models supporting Security Asstertion Markup Language (SAML) based authorization are under research.

4.1.2.2 Globus Toolkit

The Globus Project is developing fundamental technologies needed to build computational grids. The major working areas of Globus Toolkit include:

Resource Management Globus Toolkit is developing uniform and scalable mechanisms for naming, locating, and allocating computational and communication resources in distributed systems. Data Management and Access. They have launched a collaborative effort to design and produce an infrastructure-level architecture for data management, which is called the data grid.

Application Development Environments The integration of Grid services into existing application development frameworks, environments, and languages (e.g., Common Object Request Broker, The Java Toolkit, Message Passing Interface).

Information Services Requirements, designs, and prototypes of a Grid information service, an enabler for dynamic application configuration and adaptation is developed in this area.

Security Security algorithms for secure group communications, management of trust relationships, and developing new mechanisms for fine-grained access control are the major topics in this working area.

Version two of the toolkit has been adopted and further developed by the EU DataGrid project [86]. While the Globus Toolkit itself does not limit how virtual organizations can be constructed and how dynamically resources and users can be added such constraints had been added by DataGrid in order to make a wide deployment and production oriented usage feasible. The chosen VO model had been rather similar to the original UNICORE model with a rather static collaboration of providers with a dynamic allocation of the concrete resources to be used for a job.

The intermediate version three of the toolkit has not been used widely as the underlying Open Grid Service Infrastructure (OGSI) concept has been discontinued and replaced by WS-RF. The WS-RF compliant version four is currently used by a wide range of research projects for their prototypes but has not yet achieved a similarly wide deployment as previous versions. In particular the successors of the DataGrid project have chosen to move their production environment towards gLite (see section 4.1.2.3) instead of the new Globus Versions.

The most recent version is used as of now in a couple of research projects and investigated in particular for its ability to support dynamic virtual organisations [19], the integration with data management solutions such as Open Grid Service Architecture-Data Access and Integration (OGSA-DAI) [87, 64].

4.1.2.3 gLite

Based on the work of the DataGrid project [86] adopting GT2 to their needs in the successor projects Enabling Grids for E-Science (EGEE) and EGEE-II a new middleware, gLite [88, 89] has been developed. The gLite middleware is web service driven and relies on a rather limited profile of Web Service standards.

While gLite from a technological viewpoint does not limit the VO model that can be applied the typical usage is also a static collaboration model whereas providers are pre-selected or conditions are negotiated out of band. This gLite middleware is widely used in production Grid environments and has achieved a high level of maturity. Additionally it supports the operation of several VOs in parallel and the inclusion of resources in more than one VO at a time.

4.1.2.4 Grid based Aggregated Service Provision

The EU Grid based Application Service Provision (GRASP) project [90, 29, 40, 41, 28, 91] has been one of the pioneering projects experimenting with the use Grid computing in order for the support and operation of the provision of 'software as a service'. The evaluation of the sustainability of new models of Application Service Provision (ASP) towards a so called Aggregated Service provision has been investigated.

In order to support the ASP models outlined above the GRASP infrastructure has introduced additional services to the one proposed in the Open Grid Service Infrastructure [76] specification.

Orchestration One of the most important aspects of the new ASP models is that no longer one single vendor controls the whole process. This means that a mechanism is needed that orchestrate the services offered by different vendors and ensure a controlled collaboration. The GRASP orchestration service will be based on BPEL4WS and provide the possibility for a hybrid orchestration for Grid Services but also for Web Services.

SLA Monitoring The Orchestrator can only fulfil its task in controlling the collaboration between the different services if enough information for the decision process is avail-able. The SLA monitoring services monitor, enforce and provide notifications in order to assist the Orchestrator in this task.

Accounting & Billing Without Accounting & Billing no Application Service Provision can be performed. As the services are no longer controlled by one single entity but from many different service providers over time new ways on collecting provided services must be introduced. Especially for the "many-to-many" model new solutions must be identified.

Within the GRASP project the notion of the Virtual Hosting Environment (VHE) has been introduced hiding internal management and re-scheduling activities from the consumer while maintaining the validity of the external resource reference identifiers (called Service Locators). This new concept combined with a model for the realisation of SLAs beyond purely Quality of Service parameters has been used as starting point for the framework described in chapter 5.

4.1.2.5 Grid for Industrial Applications

The Grid for Industrial Applications (GRIA) middleware originated from a European Research project in the 5th framework programme in parallel to the GRASP project described in the previous section. The software has been further developed in several European research projects such as Grids for Industrial Product Development (SIMDAT) and The Next Generation Grid (NextGrid). The GRIA middleware is based on the SOA paradigm and is assuming site-autonomy and is driven by commercial scenarios where the resource sharing must be configurable in a rather fine grained way. The implementation has been done based on Web Service technology and Public Key Infrastructure (PKI). Figure 4.3 shows the fundamental architecture of the GRIA system.

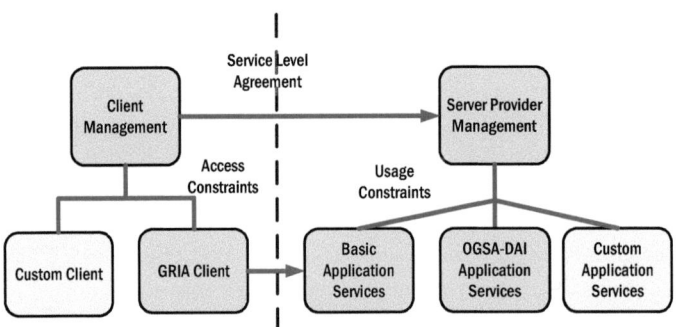

Figure 4.3: GRIA fundamental architecture

The interaction between clients and providers is based on an Service Level Agreement (SLA) that need to be managed on the server but also on the client side. The assumption is that obligations in the SLA are also covering the client side as in an SLA where a certain response time is guaranteed comes typically along with limit for the number of requests in a given time period. Consequently the client would need to control that the number of requests are not exceeded. The GRIA architecture as shown in figure 4.3 is designed to be open for inclusions of custom applications on the server as on the client side.

4.2 Information Models and Management Protocols

The basis for an autonomous management solution is a well defined information model that allows communicating and exchanging the status of a monitored entity between different management components. The following sections discuss existing standards or specifications from other publications that exist.

4.2.1 GLUE

The GLUE[2] Schema provides in [92, 93] an information model to provide the necessary information about the resources available in a Grid environment and supports the sharing of resources across several Virtual Organisation (VO). The use cases [94] collected as driver for the specification clearly indicate a focus of the specification for a VO that is built from a set of rather homogeneous set of resources. Additionally it is also assumed that the focus is on the sharing of resources and that the provision of internal status information is possible.

While the assumed collaboration model is in contradiction of the VO model proposed in this thesis and is seen not in line with the SOA paradigm of virtualization of resources the model is seen as quite complete and is clearly applicable for the service provider internal resource description for HPC providers.

4.2.2 SNMP

The Simple Network Management Protocol (SNMP) protocol has been designed for the monitoring and management of network components and originates from the Internet Engineering Task Force (IETF) standards body. SNMP is a quite simple protocol with only five message directives. The SNMP architecture proposes *Agents* that maintain a set of management information (name and type) following the specific format described in a Management Information Base (MIB). The

---
[2] The original meaning was Grid Laboratory Uniform Environment but it is no longer used

information is organised in a hierarchical manner with unique identifiers. The defined message directives are

GetRequest is sent from the *Manager* to the *Agent* in order to request the values of one or more status variables

GetNextRequest is sent from the *Manager* to the *Agent* requesting the next value considering the enumeration of values as defined in the MIB

SetRequest is sent from the *Manager* to the *Agent* in order to set a value

GetResponse is sent from the *Agent* to the *Manager* as a response to one of the two possible GetRequests

Trap is used by the *Agent* in order to inform the *Manager* about exceptions. The message is issued without a preceding request message from the *Manager*

SNMP is widely used in particular for the monitoring of network and low level system parameters and is widely supported by vendors. The communication is realised as a simple connectionless protocol on the transport layer leading to a quite good performance in comparison to connection oriented protocols such as Common Management Information Protocol (CMIP) (see below). A major issue related to SNMP is the rather simple security model and the performance degradations for very large MIBs.

4.2.3 DMI

The Desktop Management Interface (DMI) specification was targeting at a standard framework for managing and tracking components in a desktop pc, notebook or server. The specification aimed to address the gap between management software and the system's components. The DMI has been designed to be:

- independent of a specific computer, operating system or management protocol
- easy for vendors to adopt
- usable locally and via the network using different kind of protocols
- integrated with other management protocols such as CMIP and SNMP

The DMI specification was discontinued in 2005 and has been integrated in the Component Information Model (CIM) set of specifications (see section 4.2.5).

4.2.4 CMIP

The Common Management Information Protocol (CMIP) [95] is an Open Systems Interconnection (OSI)-based network management protocol standard that supports information exchange between network management applications and management agents. Its design is similar to the Simple Network Management Protocol (SNMP). A detailed comparison of SNMP and CMIP is provided in [96].

CMIP is based on the OSI protocol stack and is consequently a connection-oriented protocol. This restricts the usage of CMIP on components with the necessary resources to allow a complete implementation of layer 1-3 of the OSI stack. Based on this high demand an alternative implementation called CMIP over TCP/IP (CMOT) has been specified in [97]. This enables the usage of CMIP also on TCP/IP based networks.

The CMIP information model is object oriented and the CMIP Machine (CMIPM) is similar to the *Manager* in the SNMP architecture and is sending requests to the *Agents*. While the information model is quite complex and powerful the protocol had been kept relatively simple very similar to the one discussed above for SNMP. CMIP is also used so far only quite narrowly in the telecommunications sector.

4.2.5 CIM

the Component Information Model (CIM) is a specification of the Distributed Management Task Force (DMTF). The purpose of the specification as outlined in [98] is to establish a common conceptual framework that describes the managed environment. The model, expressed in the Unified Modeling Language (UML) is seen as a unification of existing models realised with the Management Information Base (MIB) used in Simple Network Management Protocol (SNMP) and the Desktop Management Interface (DMI) and Common Management Information Protocol (CMIP) models. The model is defined independently from the way the information is retrieved or stored.

The major advantage of CIM compared e.g. to the flat information model expressed in MIBs is the possibility to express relations such as inheritance or other dependencies. The key innovations of CIM compared to other information models are

- Reduced complexity of the models based on the performed abstraction and classification of the problem domain defining high level and fundamental concepts, common characteristics and their relationships as baseline for the specific objects
- Utilization of object oriented concepts such as object inheritance or the use of associations to depict relationships between the objects

- Use of semantic annotations of the associations allowing to express common characteristics and features
- Definition of abstract behaviour such as *Reset* or *Reboot* independent of the underlying hardware
- Common model across the whole management environment covering System, Device, Network, User, Application, and potentially custom defined other problem spaces

4.2.6 MIMO

In [99] a generic monitoring solution for middleware is described. This architecture has proven its usability in different application scenarios (see for example [100]). The approach is focused on monitoring and addresses already the need for monitoring on different levels of a distributed application ranging from hardware, network, and middleware up to the application level. However the approach is based on Common Object Request Broker which limits the usability of the approach in commercial settings as firewalls makes the communication via CORBA difficult. The used platforms are very often not equipped with CORBA.

4.2.7 Grid Monitoring Architecture

The basic idea of the Grid Monitoring Architecture [101] specification was to address the problem of a large number of non interoperable monitoring solutions for grids [102, 103, 104, 105]. The key difference to other monitoring specifications the need for operating across organisational boundaries and the need for a high level of scalability was identified. The Grid Monitoring Architecture (GMA) components identified are the event producer, event consumer and so called intermediary components (as shown in figure 4.4).

This intermediary component allow the realisation of monitoring hierarchies moving from the monitoring from raw monitored data such as cpu usage up to more higher level data that allows the communication of data outside the organisation to the other collaborators in a more coarse grained way.

4.2.7.1 R-GMA

The Relational Grid Monitoring Architecture (R-GMA) [106] architecture is based on the GMA approach outlined in the previous section and is relying on relational databases to store the data.

4.2 Information Models and Management Protocols

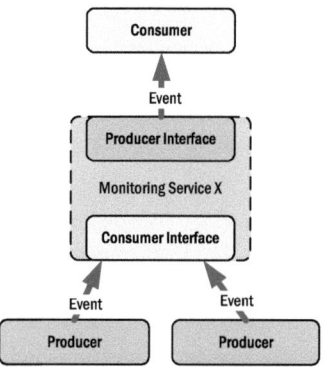

Figure 4.4: GMA compound producer and consumer concept

R-GMA has been developed as part of the EGEE project and is widely used in EGEE based Virtual Organisations.

The R-GMA approach is based on the simple model expressed in the GMA work but it adds some more concrete roles for producer, consumers and intermediaries. This includes archiving nodes that stores the monitored information in databases for later queries and is relying on a hierarchical model having a data collection layer, a data archiving layer and a external access layer.

The model is quite similar to the concepts expressed in the Management Using Web Services (MUWS) specification (see below). However the implementation is done using proprietary protocols and the query language is SQL.

4.2.7.2 Web Service Level Agreements

The Web Service Level Agreement (WSLA) specification [107] is not the result of a standardisation body but is a concept driven by IBM. The WSLA concept specifically addresses only distributed applications that are built using Web Services technology. As a consequence the subject of supervision is the relationship between a single service consumer and a service provider environment. So before a service consumer consumes the service provided a Service Level Agreement (SLA) needs to be negotiated between the two involved parties. The Service Level Agreement is expressed in machine readable eXtensible Meta Language. It is explicitly foreseen that a federated model where a service provider do not provide the full service itself but uses further services provided from different service provider is supported. In this scenario the service provider acts as a consumer of

Chapter 4 State of the Art and Relevant Standards

the services and service provider at the same time. Furthermore a client server model is assumed as precondition where a service provider environment is aware of all SLAs agreed to service consumers and is able to do local optimisation (e.g. for not violating the SLA or intentionally violating an SLA in order to fulfil another, from a business objectives point of view, more important SLA). The SLA itself do not only contain the metrics that must be fulfilled but also specific actions to be taken in case of violation and also supports the generation of events e.g. up to the workflow level in order to apply certain actions on SLA violation(s). The management of the SLAs is done in a hierarchical manner. On the lowest level there are Measurement Services maintaining information on the current system configuration and runtime configuration on the low level metrics that are part of the SLA. This measurement can be either from inside by retrieving the metrics directly for example retrieved via Simple Network Management Protocol or Component Information Model (see above) or from outside by probing or intercepting client transactions. The Condition Evaluation Services is responsible for monitoring compliance of the SLA parameters and the metrics gained by the Measurement Services. This evaluation is either on a regular time basis or on event basis. In case of violations of the SLA the kind of violation is transmitted to a Management Services in order to start corrective actions. This provider oriented concept allows a harmonised reaction on SLAs based on different business objectives. However the optimisation for the distributed application is not possible in this way. So it is at the moment not foreseen that an agent aiming at supervising a distributed simulation has to consider objectives of other parallel distributed simulations utilising partly the same resources.

4.2.7.3 Generic System Supervision

Within the European research project GeneSyS a Web Service based solution had been realised for the application domain of distributed interactive simulations. The simulation based on Run-Time-Infrastructure (RTI) was amended by a control plane utilizing at this time emerging Web Service technology. The basic architecture as shown in figure ?? and as defined by the author with contribution from other project partners in [30] proposes a framework based on several *Communication Server CORE* and different type of Agents connected to the *CORE* via a specific *GeneSyS Connector*.

Beside the obvious Monitoring Agent realising an interface to the Monitored Entity for providing access to the status data and the operations to manipulate it several utility services are necessary. The Directory Server is used in for the discovery of Monitoring Agents for a specific Monitored Entity. The Repository stores the data of the sessions for a later analysis. Other possible additional agents foreseen perform a filtering of the data (for example for different roles of supervisors) and

4.2 Information Models and Management Protocols

Summarizer address the need for reducing the load on the network by providing not all data to external agents but only e.g. average values.

All these components are ultimately participating to allow supervisors using a Console Agent to analyse the distributed simulation and to perform one or more of the available operations on the Monitored Entity. Such operations might aim to solve certain problems without interrupting the operation (for example reducing the resolution of the video stream in case of bandwidth problems) or pause the distributed application until again a 'green' system state can be reached.

In order to ease the task of the supervisor the messages communicated via the Core are already pre-processed and do not only contain the raw data itself but have been already compared to given boundaries indicating the error status. Additionally the data must not be provided in a continuous fashion but can be triggered to by only submitted on such a threshold miss. This event based communication where in case of an error free operation on messages are sent required the introduction of a self-monitoring mechanism that provided a regular heartbeat message in order to proof liveliness of the component.

Further details on GeneSyS can be found in the following publications of the author and others [31, 32, 33, 34].

4.2.7.4 Management using Web Services (MUWS)

The Management Using Web Services (MUWS) specification [108] is one of the results of the OASIS working group on Web Service Distributed Management (WSDM). While the specification has started using vanilla Web Services the final specifications had been aligned with the results of the OASIS-WSRF group. Within this group the Web Service Resource Framework (WSRF) have been defined. This clearly indicates that MUWS is targeting for Service Oriented Grids.

As shown in [108, 109] the MUWS architecture is service oriented and solves the problem of aligning functional and management elements of a service by introducing specific *portTypes* for management additionally to the functional elements of the interface. The concept foresees a *Managed Resource* that is exposed through a *Manageability Provider* (in figure 4.5 the triangle at the boundary of the dashed box). The properties of this *Managed Resource* are consumed by *Manageability Consumers*. The consumer monitors and controls the Managed Resources.

The realisation of a *Managed Resource* can be done either by a direct instrumentation realising a directly *Manageable Resource* or via a *Management Agent*.

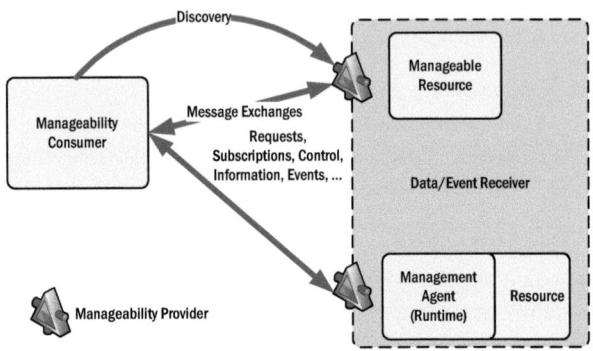

Figure 4.5: MUWS Architecture

4.2.7.5 Web Based Enterprise Management

The Web Based Enterprise Management (WBEM) set of specifications cover the WS-Transfer, WS-Enumeration and WS-Management specifications [79] as a transport mechanism using Web Services based on the Component Information Model (CIM) information model. However the WBEM group is also working on a mapping on the MUWS specifications and as mentioned before the convergence of WS-RF (used for MUWS) and the WS-Management, WS-Enumeration and WS-Transfer specifications is already announced.

4.2.7.6 Nagios

Nagios [110] is a system and network monitoring application and allows the reporting of errors for a wide range of system parameters. It comes with a large number of plug-ins but is designed to be extensible. All plug-ins can deliver their values to a remote server using the Nagios Remote Plug-In Executor (NRPE) concept.

The data collection is either triggered by the Nagios server system (e.g. every 5 minutes) or is triggered by an external application that typically is installed on the monitored entity pushing the info towards the Nagios server. The foreseen use of the collected information is via a web interface indicating the status of the services using a kind of dashboard display.

4.2.7.7 Ganglia

Ganglia [12] is a scalable (so far up to 2000 compute nodes) distributed monitoring system specifically designed for monitoring of cluster systems. It is designed to support multiple clusters at a time. The communication between the Ganglia daemons (gmond) is realised using a multicast based listen/announce protocol for the heartbeat messages across the nodes and a tree based point-to-point connections amongst representative cluster nodes for an aggregation of their state as shown in figure 4.6.

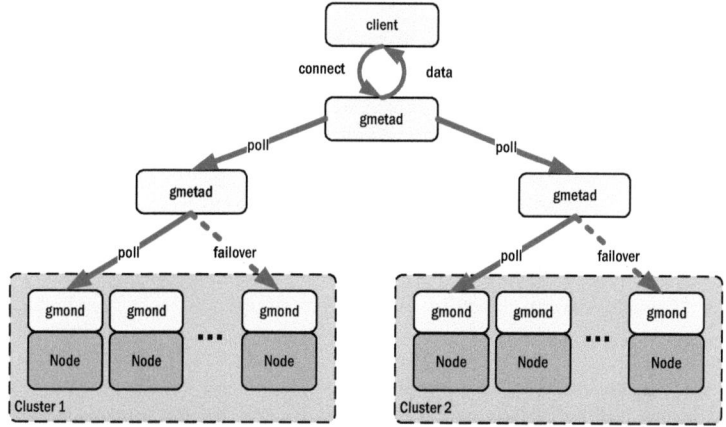

Figure 4.6: The Ganglia architecture [12]

The data structure is not following any of the information model standards mentioned above but defines a proprietary XML based data format with the goal of a low footprint on the monitored nodes. Beside the built-in metrics also application defined metrics are supported allowing an adaptation and extension of the monitored data set. The federation of the data from individual clusters is done by the Ganglia Meta Daemon (gmetad).

4.2.7.8 Lemon

The Lemon and the Fault Detection and Recovery (FDR) concept presented in [13] propose a mechanism for realising a monitoring and fabric management solution for computational resources.

In contrast to the Ganglia the XML protocol is only used for the control channel messages but not for the data exchange itself where a more efficient binary representation. Beside Lemon does not

Chapter 4 State of the Art and Relevant Standards

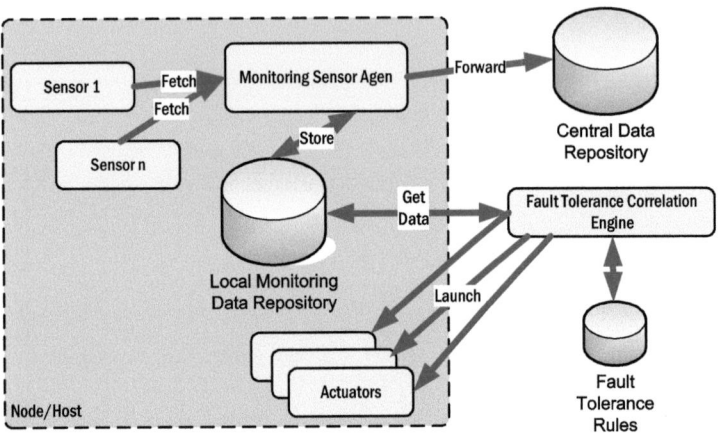

Figure 4.7: The Lemon and FDR concept [13]

foresee that all cluster nodes push the data to all other cluster nodes as in Ganglia but use a local data store that forwards the data directly to a central data store leading to a much higher efficiency in particular for larger clusters.

The monitored data can be either accessed directly via a pull or subscription model from the local repository via a defined API expressed in the Web Service Description Language (WSDL) format. The transport of monitoring data from the local entity to the central repository can also be customized. So far UDP and TCP implementations exist.

The Fault Detection and Recovery (FDR) approach is leveraging the monitoring concept to a true management framework actively influencing the system state via *Fault Tolerance Actuators* based on the *Fault Tolerance Rules* described in a proprietary XML format.

4.2.7.9 INCA

The INCA framework[3] has been developed as part of the TeraGrid project and is realising a monitoring framework for Grid end-users. The data collection on the computational resources is done by realising *Reporter* scripts that for example reports the version of the intel compiler installed or the version of a mathematical library. The concept assumes a central repository for all reporters and their automated deployment on all INCA enabled resources. The monitored results are made

---
[3]http://inca.sdsc.edu

4.2 Information Models and Management Protocols

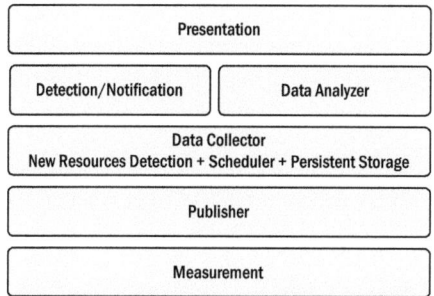

Figure 4.8: The GridICE layered architecture according to [14]

persistent in a so called *Depot*. The reports are either accessible via a Web portal or by special applications to every Grid End-User using its Grid identity and credentials.

4.2.7.10 GridICE

The GridICE monitoring framework [14] is designed for large scale grid deployments and widely used in eScience oriented infrastructure Grids. The architecture assume three major use cases for the framework (1) the VO level providing a view about the accesible resources and their configurations (e.g. software, compiler versions, etc.) (2) site level providing the necessary information for different type of sites ranging from large centres operating in a 24/7 mode up to small centres (3) the operation domains realising the Grid Operations Centre (GOC) as an intermediary between site operators and the end-users.

The GridICE framework is realised on top of existing Grid monitoring frameworks such as the Lemon Framework 4.2.7.8 but is also relying on non Grid solutions such as SNMP and the Web Based Enterprise Management standards.

The chosen architecture is organised in several layers (see 4.8) starting from a Measurement Service where the monitored entities are probed for their status. GridICE does not prescribe any particular collection mechanism or information model and has been integrated with several different toolkits and models including (SNMP, CIM, Lemon, GLUE and LDAP). The *Publisher Service* realises the access interface for external users and is similar to other frameworks as discussed above propose a common information model to be used above this point. The chosen solution is to rely on the GLUE schema and to use the Globus Meta Directory Service (MDS) version 2 as publication method. Additionally a *Data Collector* Service storing the monitoring data for analysis of historical data is foreseen. On top of this layer *Detection/Notification* and *Data Analyser* services are proposed that realises a communication framework for detected errors e.g. using Short Message Service (SMS), provide functionality assisting in the diagnosis of errors and providing performance analysis and statistics from the collected data. For the data analysis part the usage of data mining concepts using On-Line Analytical Processing (OLAP) have been investigated. The *Presentation Service* realises a web-based graphical user interface to the data.

4.2.8 Tivoli

The Tivoli framework is designed for distributed system administration, software distribution, remote configuration, remote control, remote monitoring. Its design is proprietary, thus it does not support standard protocols (like SNMP) but it can be interfaced with the IBM's network analysis product Netview in order to enhance the field of operations.

4.2.9 Unicenter (Computer Associates)

The Unicenter framework is based on a central object repository containing all devices managed by the platform. Its implementation is more open than Tivoli's as it admits the use of various protocols and allows the definition of extension modules. However it is also limited to human operator driven monitoring.

4.2.10 Openview (HP)

HP Openview is dedicated to network supervision, the Openview environment has been augmented with many functionalities linked to systems and applications. Its implementation is based on SNMP.

4.2.11 Openmaster (Evidian-Bull)

Openmaster was designed like a universal platform supporting a large field of protocols and information models (SNMP, CMIP, Network oriented. The product is focused on security purposes.

4.3 Existing Management Approaches

Additional to concepts realised in toolkits such as discussed above, also different approaches for resource, network and system management exist. As most of the toolkits are limited to a pure monitoring most of them need to be extended significantly to move towards an autonomous management system. In this section approaches for gaining knowledge from the monitored data and how management solutions could be realised are discussed.

4.3.1 Rule based Approaches

One existing approach is outlined in [111] and [112] realised by storing specific symptom-cause pairs in a database. If a monitored situation fits or is *similar* to a symptom stored in the case database the solutions for such a case can be executed. The major problem to solve in this kind of systems is defining the metrics evaluating the level of similarity for the monitored symptoms and the one stored in the database. Another critical point is the size and quality of the case database. Very often historical data for example from a trouble ticket system are used to feed such databases (see for example [113]). This kind of approach is only suitable for rather static settings and where the dependencies and interactions between the different nodes in the distributed setting are rather well understood. Of course the quality of these systems is heavily dependant on the quality of the case database and the stored measures. Another problem of the cited systems is that they operate on the low level metrics of the system which is leading to a high amount of traffic for the monitoring and also to a complex mapping of many different cases to a the same measures (e.g. many different parameters settings could indicate an *overload* situation that need to be addressed by the measure *add spare resources*.

An alternative approach is exploiting the fact that a high level of interdependency between the components from the different layers from network over system, middleware and application exist. In order to define the right measures on how to detect and react on problems in the operation of distributed applications knowledge on the topology and the dependencies of the different components is necessary. In [114] an event correlator based on dependency graphs is introduced. Using this dependency graph it is possible to identify which components of a distributed system will be affected if an error occurs. The approach is also limited to configuration where the interdependencies are well understood and rather static in order to allow maintenance of the solution with a acceptable amount of human resources.

Other correlation approaches that aim to map automatically from low level metrics to higher level error conditions are described in [115, 116] using a specific programming language or the com-

Chapter 4 State of the Art and Relevant Standards

plete distributed system is modelled in its event behaviour in [117].

Another rule based approach has been already discussed in section 4.2.7.8 and is detailed in [13]. This solution defines also a set of rules reacting on a well defined number of events and applying appropriate counter measures e.g. restarting an sshd daemon.

4.3.2 Policy Based Management

Policy-based management approaches had been developed in order to achieve a more dynamic behaviour of the management systems. The underpinning consideration is that the rule based approach used in isolation is too static for the dynamically changing environment where the IT infrastructure is continuously changed and updated. So more general policy based management aim to move the fixed rule based approaches towards a more objective and goal oriented approach. An example where policies are applied to address management challenges is outlined in [118] with a focus on security policies.

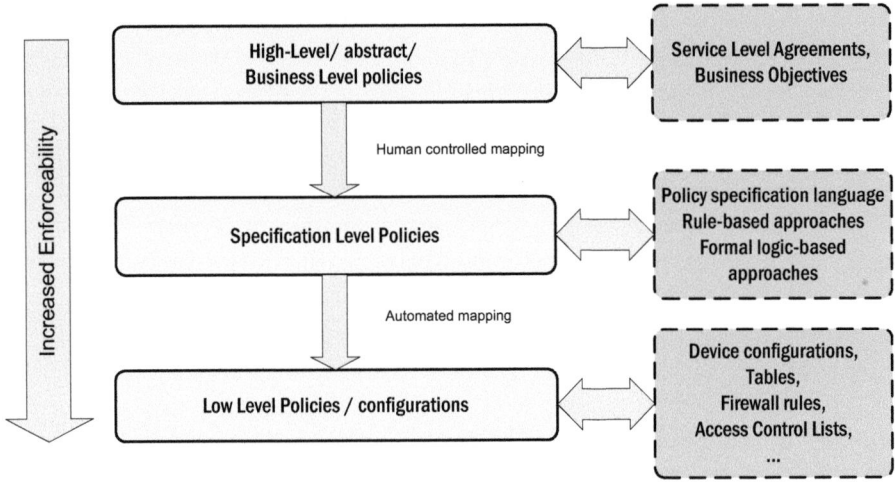

Figure 4.9: Layered approach of policy based management

In [119] the core concepts of policy based management are defined. The basic concept is that at a Policy Enforcement Point (PEP) the need for a decision is detected and that this and potentially many other PEPs communicate this decision request to one Policy Decision Point (PDP) in order to receive a decision. Of course additional elements for realising such an infrastructure are necessary such as a policy repository where all the policies used for the decision are stored.

The major difference to purely rule based approaches as discussed in the previous section is the assumption that a hierarchy of policies exists as shown in figure 4.9 from human readable high level and more abstract policies down to the level of machine readable and understandable policies. The typical assumption taken is that the initial transformation step is done using a human operator while further steps can be done automatically.

A wide range of policy languages and formal logic-based approaches do exist such as Ponder [120], Rei [121], ProPoliS [122] or eXtensible Access Control Modeling Language (XACML) [123] to name a few. A full description of them is beyond of the scope of this thesis.

4.4 Summary and Conclusions

A wide range of *monitoring* solutions exist either for the network and system level or for distributed application or Grids. Different information models exists partially standardized and lots of them proprietary.

None of these tools have been designed to support the VO model presented in chapter 2 as they are either limited to the system and hardware level or at best aim to realise a management across the site. If the solution is realised for Grids the fact that most of the information collected within a site cannot be provided to other sites or a centralized Grid Operations Centre (GOC) in the cases where an industrial usage of the resources is foreseen disqualifies all existing solutions.

None of the existing solutions is able to fulfil the requirements worked out in section 3 in particular the anticipated site autonomy and the role of the SLAs at the provider boundary as driving element for all management decisions within a site are not considered.

Requirements	Reference Numbers from chapter 3	Tools/Specifications/Standards partially supporting these requirements
Realisation of a complete status picture based on information coming from different information sources and understand their interdependencies	Req.1, Req.3, Req.10, Req.16	GeneSyS

Chapter 4 State of the Art and Relevant Standards

Requirements	Reference Numbers from chapter 3	Tools/Specifications/Standards partially supporting these requirements
Common Information Model	Req.2, Req.7	CIM, MIB, GLUE, ...
Active Management towards defined desirable system conditions	Req.4, Req.11	Policy Based Management (conceptual only)
Appropriate inclusions of humans in the management process and well defined escalation strategy	Req.5, Req.12	Typically either the management is completely done by humans and the system is reduced to a pure monitoring system or a full automation is targeted.
Support for lifecycle based management considering different goals during the handling of a complex tasks	Req.6, Req.17	The priorities and the management goals change over time depending on the phase of the task. Existing solutions assume either static rules/policies or accept only changes in the business objectives as driver for updates.
Transformation from external obligations to internal management metrics and goals	Req.8	While this is part of the vision of policy based management a full automation is still under research and is not even available on a conceptual level.
Management driven by business objectives rather then technical parameters	Req.9	Not supported by existing tools.
Support for confidentiality of monitoring information in particular across organisational boundaries	Req. 13	Some support has been realised in GridICE but cross-organisational management is anticipated as non-goal for most other solutions.

4.4 Summary and Conclusions

Requirements	Reference Numbers from chapter 3	Tools/Specifications/Standards partially supporting these requirements
Resolution of potential discrepancies of external defined management goals and site specific goals	Req.14	Not supported as if cross-organisational monitoring or management is considered a collaborative mood of all participants is anticipated
Differentiation between replaceable and essential resources	Req.15	problem is solved by putting such rules into SLA specifications

Table 4.1: Requirements mapped on available standards and technologies

In summary on can say that a rich set of tools and specifications are available for monitoring the state of systems, networks, clusters or any other kind of hardware. Additionally different approaches are available to instrument software services in order to make information about their state available. While many tools are using non-standardized information models a transformation from this proprietary formats into the available 'common' data formats such as CIM or GLUE are feasible. The big gap identified in the table above between the high level, more abstract, management goals and the available metrics from the software and hardware is conceptually close by policy based management approaches proposing a kind of 'magic' mapping process from a Business Management Layer down to a Resource Control Layer using the terminology introduced in [124].

Chapter 5

Monitoring and Management Concepts

In the previous chapter one of the key result of the state of the art analysis was that there is a wide range of systems for *monitoring* the state of (distributed) systems. Additionally existing monitoring solutions for Grid environments designed for large scale deployments are already available but do not meet essential requirements identified in chapter 3. This is related to the different viewpoint of these projects on the Virtual Organisation concept as a mechanism for sharing resources for achieving a common purpose rather then the economically driven viewpoint presented in chapter 2.

Additionally the view that all relations within the Virtual Organisation need to be documented and controlled by Service Level Agreements do not allow on one hand to have a centralized approach for the monitoring but enable and require on the other hand the active *management* of the resources in order to fulfil these SLAs. Consequently a different approach is needed for the realisation of an appropriate monitoring and management framework.

In the first part of this chapter a set of terms are introduced that can be used further on as they are used in slightly different meanings in different publications. Utilizing these definitions a conceptual architecture is presented. The chapter is concluded with a discussion of the applicability of existing management methods on the different layers in this concept.

5.1 Concepts and Terminology

A wide range of terms are used for describing monitoring and management solutions and very often the meaning in literature is not consistent. The understanding within this thesis is listed in the following table:

Chapter 5 Monitoring and Management Concepts

Term	Description
Instrumentation	In order to collect information from the resources different approaches might be necessary. For some resources no direct metering of the values could be possible and the desired information must be extracted from log files or by applying a patch to the software. Similar for applying corrective measures on a resource an appropriate interface must be realised. The enabling of resources to be manageable is called Instrumentation.
Metering	Based on the instrumentation mechanism one can measure the resource utilization. This data collection is called Metering
Monitoring	Based on the collected raw data from the Metering components the information is converted to a standard format or is aggregated from several values (cpu usage, memory utilization, ...) in order to fill an information record e.g. on system load. The aggregation can be also a summary across several resources such as the average number of requests for a web server farm instead of individual load values or can be an integration across layers combining information from network with system load.
Supervision	Supervision is the usage of the monitoring information and potentially a set of pre-defined or individual counter measures. This counter measures are selected and triggered by a human operator. This concept already needs the instrumentation part for influencing a situation actively but no automated mechanisms are in place.
Management	Management is understood as the mechanism of collecting information from a potentially large number of monitoring resources and their automated analysis. The analysis might find an appropriate measure and apply this measure on the resources in order to overcome the situation. Management components can be hierarchical. This means that if a local management component cannot find a solution for addressing the problem it can be escalated to a higher layer. Additionally applied measures or detected critical situations are propagated to higher layers that can potentially overrule local decisions. Similar to the Supervision case the ultimate point of escalation might be a human operator.

Table 5.1: Definition of used terms

Beyond the level of management as described in the table above there are ongoing research work in the realisation of an organic computing[1] or fully self-management capable systems that are able to learn and adapt to fully unforeseen situations and ultimately render any human intervention to be unnecessary. For this thesis this kind of management has been considered not to be applicable (yet) for the requirements as discussed in chapter 3 and is also not in line with the concept of hard guarantees expressed in the SLAs between providers and consumers.

5.2 Conceptual View

Using the definitions from table 5.1 an initial architecture and its key building blocks can be provided. Figure 5.1 show these blocks of a management solution in line with the identified requirements from chapter 3 and suitable for commercial oriented Virtual Organisations as presented in chapter 2.

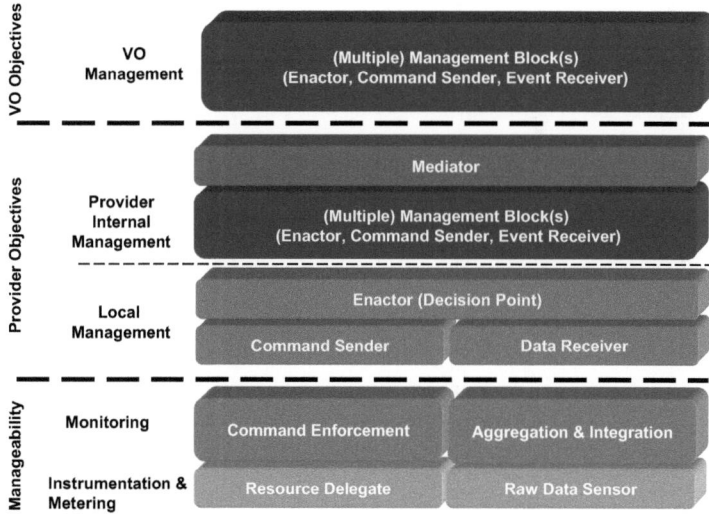

Figure 5.1: Conceptual View of the Management Framework

The management stack is divided into three major layers (indicated by the dashed line). The lowest layer enables the manageability of the resource. This layer enables the management by adding

---
[1] http://www.organic-computing.de/spp

Chapter 5 Monitoring and Management Concepts

hooks for the information collection (called *Raw Data Sensors*) and for influencing the configuration (called *Resource Delegate*). On top of this instrumentation and metering layer the monitoring layer acts as a an aggregator and integrator of the information. Major role of the *Aggregation & Integration* component is the realisation of a common data and communication format for the higher layers and to reduce the overall amount of information that need to be exchanged. So consequently at the boundary of the manageability layer a common information and data model can be assumed independently from the large variety of different data collection methods and the used tools on the instrumentation and metering layer.

The middle layer represents the provider internal management framework that might be organised in a hierarchical manner as indicated in figure 5.1. So while only two layers are shown there is no conceptual limitation implied. Between this middle layer and the VO management wide management a mediator component is acting as a filter for the information flow and external requests. Within this layer the assumption is that full control of the underlying resources is given.

The VO Management layer is responsible for the cross-provider management. As outlined above the communication between this layer and the potentially large number of providers is mediated. An important consequence of this is the lack of *control* about the provided services. Every provider remains completely autonomous. This is, as said before, in contradiction to current practice in many Grid infrastructures and is also the major reasons why existing solutions cannot be re-used for a VO wide management.

5.2.1 Manageability Layer

This part is seen as a component very tightly integrated with the monitored resource and is expected to show a quite minimalistic footprint. As discussed in chapter 4 a wide range of solutions for this purpose exist such as Nagios [110, 125], Lemon [13] just to name a few. Most of the tools analysed use a push communication model providing information on the status of the monitored entity on a regular basis but also the pull model is commonly available. The advantage of the pull model is that the time of the request can be aligned with the main activities of the monitored entity. An example would be to query a compute node of a cluster between two jobs and not during a compute intensive activity.

As outlined in chapter 4 many tools do not foresee the collected information to by automatically processed but push the information to scripts hosted in a web server. These scripts produce colourful reports or status dashboards as indicator of the system status for a human operator. Quite commonly the information shown just covers the overall situation and allow in case of error conditions to query for details (moving from the push to the pull model). A human operator

5.2 Conceptual View

can easily cope with a set of different tools and their quite heterogeneous and diverging way to display the monitored information. The goal of an automated management can only be realised if this information collection is mapped on a common information model such as proposed by the Distributed Management Task Force (DMTF) with the Component Information Model (CIM). The author and others have proposed a simple information model for distributed applications in [30].

5.2.1.1 Integrated Sensor

The most efficient way to provide access to the externally relevant part of internal system state is by adding a specific interface to the process, component or hardware. As outlined in chapter 4 this could be the Simple Network Management Protocol (SNMP) with its GET, SET and TRAP commands, the Java Management Extensions (JMX) or proprietary hook mechanisms. Of course it is also possible to add any proprietary mechanism to query for the necessary data. Many applications allow this approach by providing hooks into the processing chain e.g. the filter mechanisms of many web servers.

5.2.1.2 Indirect Sensor

Unfortunately very often there is no direct access to the system state information. If the monitored entity is a software process one might be able to parse log files or monitor the process with operating system capabilities (e.g. memory consumption). In some cases where no internal information is stored one can only perform a kind of 'black-box' testing. As an example a component could measure the average response time for a web page of known size from web server in order to provide an indicator for the current load situation. This external detection method is very often the only possible solution for hardware components. The realisation of such indirect sensors is commonly done using wrappers that provide externally the same interface as realised for Integrated Sensors but instead of having direct access to the internal state they perform an approach similar to the ones mentioned above. The indirect approach does not only have drawbacks. While the access to the system state is more complicated the monitoring is not located on the same physical entity and has less influence on the operation. So in case of failures of the monitored entity an integrated sensor might be affected at the same time. So in general it is advisable to combine both approaches and have integrated and indirect sensors for a monitored entity.

Chapter 5 Monitoring and Management Concepts

5.2.1.3 Aggregation and Integration

Very often the individual data and state of a single resource is not relevant and it is sufficient to communicate an average value. Very often such a value provide more information as a snapshot at a certain point in time. So it is advisable to consolidate the information from the continuous monitoring in order to minimize the information flood. The *Aggregator* component is responsible for collecting the information and transforms it to a significantly reduced amount of information. A simple scenario demonstrating how sensor components and an aggregator component work together is shown in figure 5.2. In this sample a server farm of web services is monitored (e.g. by an integrated sensor implemented as a filter). The sensor perform a local aggregation from values such as cpu usage, free disk space and other parameters to an overall system status of 'green', 'yellow' or 'red' and pushes this state to the *Aggregator* component hosted on a separate server. The operator monitoring this farm is in a different network (or even somewhere in the Internet) and does not want to have the individual information in case of an overall 'green' state. The simple *Aggregator* component in this case indicates as overall situation of the system the worst individual system state. So instead of five data packets on the individual state only one is sent.

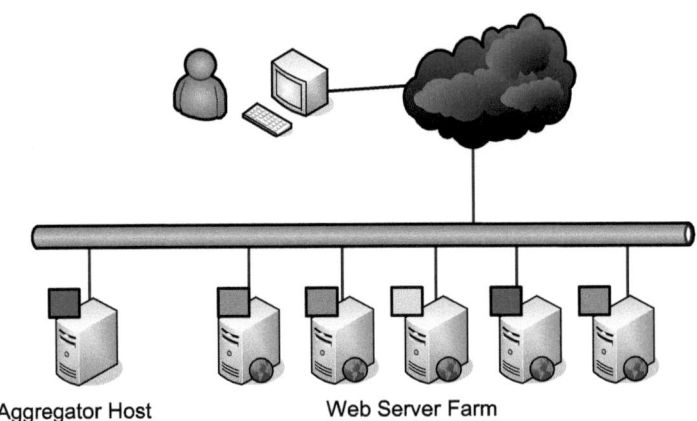

Figure 5.2: a simple monitoring scenario

If the overall system state is 'green' the operator does not take any actions. If the *Aggregator* indicates 'red' or 'yellow' the operator might query for detailed information (note that the query would go to the *Aggregator* and *not* to the potentially already overloaded web server). In case the failure persists the necessary actions could be taken to overcome the situation e.g. add additional spare

5.2 Conceptual View

resources to the server farm or remove the broken server from the farm for a detailed inspection. The implementation of such a behaviour requires the *Resource Delegate* explained below.

An important aspect as mentioned before for an automated management is the realisation of a common information model. This does not need to be standardised but must be on this level only common within the provider domain. Additionally the collected information and data from different tools and from different levels (e.g. network, system, middleware, applications, ...) need to be integrated. So in contrast to the human operator (supervision) scenario described in the previous section it is not feasible to directly consume the data in tool specific formats but a transformation into a common format is done. This integration is not yet driven by a semantic analysis but is limited to a grouping of single data chunks representing a complete system state of the monitored entity.

5.2.1.4 Sensor Cache and History

If such additional requests for detailed information are common a cache for the received individual sensor information data allows an efficient access to the data. Instead of blocking a request until new data is pushed by the sensors a request can be served from the cached values. If the cache is made persistent and for example a database is used also historical data analysis or interfacing other parts of the infrastructure (e.g. an accounting system) is possible.

The persistent storage of historical data is also essential for a proper analysis of a situation. So the cache and history component is seen as an utility component for higher layers of the management concept. For example if a significantly reduced response time is quite common between 11am and 1pm the monitoring of a such a situation is likely not to be reported as 'red' but as 'yello'. If the same situation happens at 4am in the morning a different result of the assessment can be expected. For such an assessment the historical load situation of the last days, weeks and months builds the necessary basis.

5.2.1.5 Command Enforcement

In order to allow a management component of the higher layers to receive and analyse the presented integrated information and take decisions based on them all necessary elements are described in the previous parts of this section. But for implementing the commands one need a component that is aware of the underlying resources and can translate the command in individual commands. Considering again the web server case the command 'put server 4 on hold and perform an in-depth analysis' would result in a couple of commands removing server 4 from the pool, triggering the start and execution of an in-depth analysis, collection of the result data and provision of the result data again to the management layer. The coordinated implementation of a management command is the task of the *Command Enforcement Component*.

5.2.1.6 Resource Delegate

The resource delegate is the component that is able to implement a set of commands for a certain resource. The realisation of such a component is not possible for all monitored entities and the possibility to realise it similarly as outlined above for the integrated sensor with direct access to the system is rather uncommon. Additionally there must be no direct relation between the monitored entity that indicated a problem and the place the command aiming to fix the problem is applied. Using again the above mentioned example of the server farm the reaction on the overload situation for the web servers could go to the web servers instructing them to prioritise requests from certain IP Addresses solving the problem only for this VIP address range. Another approach might be to activate more server instances for serving web requests. In the latter case the command would not go to the web servers but to a server management component.

5.2.2 Provider Internal Management Layers

Enabled by the manageability layer providing a well defined data format the information about the system state the management layers can operate independent from the underlying tools or sensors used to collect the information. Additionally the flood of information available from the large number of different sources is already significantly reduced as not all individual data but already derived information such as average values are communicated. As described above dedicated resources are provided to perform this aggregation & integration and also to realise a data cache for historical data and provide a persistence layer for the monitored data in general.

The provider internal management layer contains one ore more management blocks consisting out of a *Data/Event Receiver, Command Sender* and an *Enactor* component. The *Event Receiver* consumes the information provided from lower management layers or if the lowest layer is reached from the Manageability layer. The full chain is utilizing and relying on a standarized event format within the provider domain. The *Enactor* component take decisions and communicate them using the *Command Sender* component to the lower layer. All decisions taken are communicated in parallel up one layer. The highest internal layer in the chain does not communicate directly to the VO Management layer as shown in figure 5.1 but is supported by a *Mediator* component responsible for the external communication. This management block is inspired by the the ba-

5.2 Conceptual View

sic components of policy based management approaches (more details can be found in [52, 126]) where the Policy Decision Point (PDP) takes decisions based on received events and the Policy Enforcement Point (PEP) where the events are received *and* enforced.

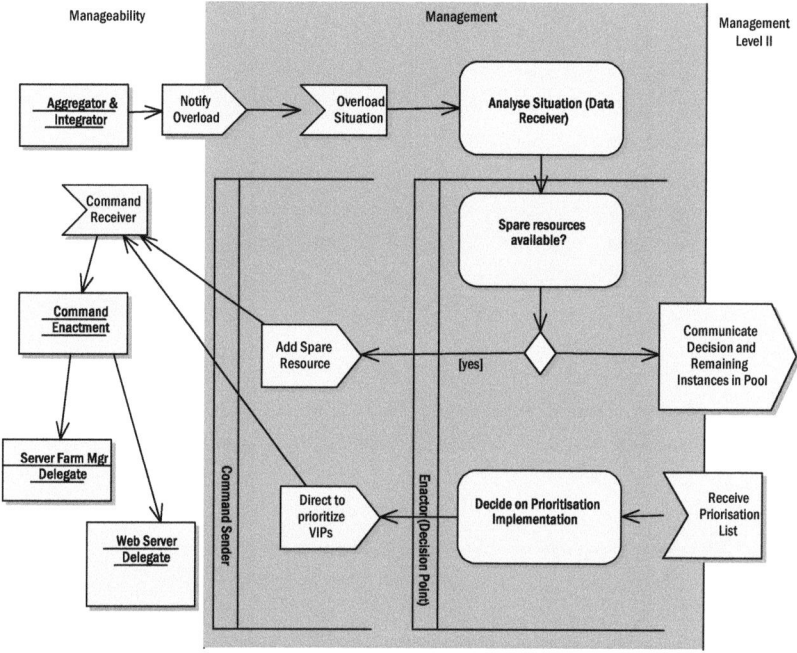

Figure 5.3: Simplified management flow for the web server farm scenario

The motivation for such a hierarchical approach having several management blocks is mainly driven by scalability, resilience and robustness considerations. That such an approach delivers an increased resilience compared to a centralized solution is straight forward. Having several autonomous components in the chain that act independent from each other enable the operation of the overall system even if certain components fail. In such situations only a reduced robustness of the system is experienced. However there is no guaranteed robustness of the system in general. Each of the layers aim to realise with the issued commands a compensating effect on the detected malfunctions and the hierarchical approach can be seen as an attempt to linearise the problem but brings at the same time the problem that the local context of the *Enactor* components might lead to wrong decisions. This problem is addressed by the communication protocol that all taken decisions are escalated (with the ultimate escalation point of a human operator) but for scalability reasons decisions need to be local. From a scalability viewpoint it is reasonable to increase also the complexity of the decision processes within the *Enactor* component going up the hierarchy. While *Local Enactor* components might be based on simple tables mapping an event with one or more commands to be executed, higher layers could be realised with rule based solutions up to flexible policy driven management approaches that potentially need a large number of information sources (in particular non-technical information such as a customer profile database). Together with this increased complexity comes a longer decision time. Table 5.2 lists a set of methods and corresponding decision times. In figure 5.3 a simple decision tree for the web server farm scenario is shown covering a scenario where some management decisions can be taken locally (activate additional server instances) up to the point where no server instances are left. At this point the higher management layers are asked for a prioritization list for the traffic that VIP customers originating from a specific IP address range can be prioritized at the web server level.

5.2.2.1 Data/Event Receiver

The *Data/Event Receiver* processes the information in the tool and collection mechanism independent format provided by the manageability layer. This component is responsible for the assessment of the conceived status and aims to map it into a category of events or errors. So additionally to the tasks already performed in the layer below a semantically driven analysis is done that could, re-using the previous example, consider that a high load situation at 4am in the morning is uncommon and indicates and error whereas the same situation at 2pm is quite normal.

A plethora of methods for the assessment of such states do exist and could be as easy as comparing the data with a set of pre-defined boundary conditions, over the detection of a negative trend (e.g. continuously decreasing performance of the IO operations) or complex algorithms e.g. self-learning approaches. There is no conceptual limitation foreseen how the assessment has to be done. Based on the assessment the Data Receiver component forward the assessment results to the *Enactor* for a decision. The right method for performing the assessment also heavily depends on the position in the management hierarchy. The closer this layer is to the monitored entity the more importance must be given to the speed of the decision time.

5.2.2.2 Enactor

The *Enactor* is the recipient of the results of the *Data/Event Receiver* and must now take a decision about the actions to be implemented. This logical block has been intentionally not called Decision Point. While it has a lot of commonality with a Policy Decision Point there are also some important differences:

5.2 Conceptual View

1. The decision is based on an integrated view considering information from different layers and sources. This means that the enforcement of the decision cannot be done at one single point but need to be delegated to a range of enforcement points that further delegate it to potentially several resources

2. The management model is hierarchical. This could be modelled with a hierarchy of PDPs. However this model is not feasible as a long hierarchy might lead to long response times and would be in contradiction with the goal to choose the optimal technology for a certain layer. The proposed alternative is that if local decisions can be taken only the decisions are communicated to higher layers that might overrule or refine them. In case a local management component cannot take a decision (or has tried several solution procedures and failed) the problem is escalated similar to the PDP chaining approach.

3. while an implementation of the decision point using policies is quite natural it is not the only possibility and would therefore constitute a quite strong limitation not appropriate for this generic level. In particular for the lower layers methods with short decision times are preferable.

So from an abstract viewpoint the *Enactor* analyses the events received from the *Data/Event Receiver* component and decides if the right measure is available to address the problem and communicate this decision to the *Command Sender* component. In parallel the decision taken together with additional data that built the basis for it are communicated to a higher management block in the form of an event message. In the Manageability layer the communication between the sensors and the aggregator/integrator is assumed to be either controlled by time intervals (e.g. every 30 seconds, every 5 minutes, ...) or by clearly identifiable events such as after every job on a compute node. As outlined above this assumption is not valid for the management layers. For an event driven communication paradigm the advantage of a substantially reduced amount of information that is transmitted comes with the drawback that a failure of a monitoring component cannot be differentiated anymore from the lack of events (indicating a good system situation). In [30, 32] the author and others proposed as solution specific heartbeat messages for all monitoring and management components realising a self-monitoring infrastructure. Other possible solutions with a smaller bandwidth footprint include the submission of events not only in case of failures but also after a pre-defined intervals or the possibility for higher management layers to request regularly a full status report.

5.2.2.3 Command Sender

This component is seen as an utility component for the *Enactor* in order not to overload this component with the task of a reliable communication to the *Command Enforcement* part of the lower layer(s). The *Enactor* provides the *Command Sender* component with the taken decision and a set of goals such as the aniticpated maximum time for a successful implementation of this decision. If the measure cannot be applied in time or not at all a corresponding event is fed back into the *Enactor* via the *Data/Event Receiver*.

5.2.2.4 Local Management Layer

This layer is special in the hierarchy of management layers as it does not receive events but only monitoring data. So the component called *Data/Event Receiver* is for this layer a pure *Data Receiver*. But more important this layer is expected to operate as interface for all management layers as interface to the monitored entities where ultimately all management decisions are enacted. For this reason it is anticipated that this layer need to implemented in a very efficient matter with extremely short decision times. In particular the implementation of commands from the higher layers (in the sample in figure 5.3 the prioritisation request) need immediate actions.

5.2.2.5 Provider Boundary Management Layer

A specific additional component at the provider boundary is the *Mediator* component. Based on the collected requirements the autonomy of a provider is one of the key elements that need to be realised and is also a key differentiator to existing VO models and existing monitoring approaches as shown in the previous chapter. The *Mediator* has some similarities to the *Aggregator & Integrator* component of the manageability layer by translating the provider internal formats into a data representation that is understood VO wide (and similarly for the external commands) but it also serves as a filter component between external entities and the internal resources. The task is a bit more complex as for different VOs different data formats and protocols must be supported. The fact that a provider is involved in several, potentially competing, VOs at a time also opens challenges related to the confidentiality of the data and requires a tight integration with the security components of the provider. It must be ensured that only the subset of the data that is eligible for a particular VO is provided to the outside for the specific role of the requestor/subscriber for this information set. Quite clear is that not all provider internal information is eligible for external entities and the acceptance of external commands will be very limited if not completely neglected.

5.2 Conceptual View

So the *Mediator* is acting as an integration, transformation and filtering component between the provider and the VO and must be tightly coupled with the security components of the provider.

5.2.3 VO Management layer

A management approach for the VO layer must consider the assumed site autonomy together with the lifecycle of VOs as discussed in chapter 2 of this thesis. Such a setting can only be operational if the conditions of the collaboration are clearly defined. These conditions embrace the complete interface ranging from connectivity up to the application service layer. Consequently it is necessary to agree on certain conditions for the provision of a service and a proper documentation of them.

For this purpose several research projects have introduced the notion of a Service Level Agreement (SLA) for services that can be negotiated and/or agreed on the fly constituting the relationship between the providers and between consumer and providers. The common understanding is that such SLAs are describing bi-partite relationships (as outlined by the author and others in [91]) between two entities or combined with a general VO agreement [52]. In [49] the author and others have shown the limitations of such approaches in highly dynamic environments.

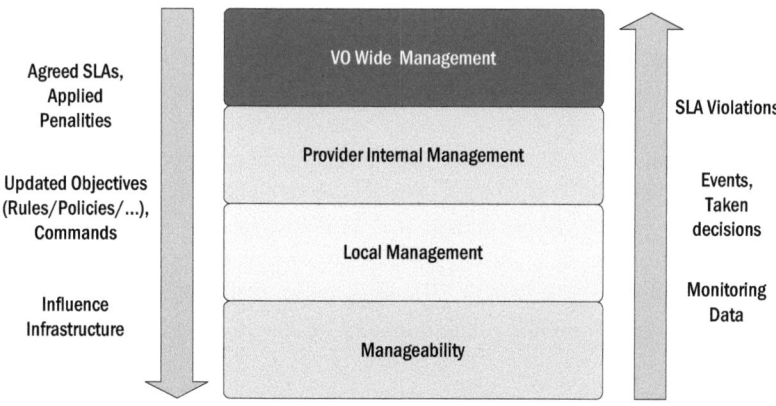

Figure 5.4: message types on the different layers

The proposed SLA model for this work has been further extended to combine the flexibility of the bi-partite approach, the consideration of legal constraints and risk mitigation from the General VO agreement approach and the identified necessity of fast SLA negotiation processes needed

Chapter 5 Monitoring and Management Concepts

in highly dynamic environments. It is proposed to limit the number of offered SLAs to a small number in order to make sure that a service provider management becomes possible. As a completely static number of SLAs would be quite inflexible the selection of possible SLAs is shifted to the preparatory phase of a Virtual Organisation. So additional to the VO lifecycle phases for the dynamic set-up of an Virtual Organisation as listed in chapter 2 some preparatory steps are necessary. Assuming that a free negotiation of SLAs is not realistic as the negotiation would take quite long, the decision process is very complex and the management of the resources to ensure the SLA cannot be based on experiences or pre-defined rules but would need to be realised in a kind of start-up process with 'learning' algorithms a substantial reduction of the complexity can be achieved. In particular in the considered cases where business scenarios are operated by the VO a free negotiation leading to a kind of 'try-and-error' management approaches would be too risky as failure in providing an SLA is typically associated with a penalty.

So in advance of setting up a collaboration within a VO either offline (e.g. a paper based contract) or in an electronic way the potential VO partners agree to a certain set of SLAs and define their properties. Also services with a lifetime beyond the lifetime of a Virtual Organisation such as service registries are filled with service descriptions including a subset of the agreed SLAs that are supported for this specific service. In [126] the author and others call this group of potential collaborators a BaseVO.

If a service of a provider has been discovered and is a potentially added to the Virtual Organisation a negotiation if a certain SLA can be provided is performed. Different negotiation protocols for this purpose do exist. Beside the proprietary approach described in [107] standardized protocols (WS-Agreement, WS-AgreementNotification) are currently in the standardization process at the OGF (Open Grid Forum). For this thesis it is sufficient to assume that by any of these protocols an agreement could be reached and this SLA must now be provided to the external consumer. For the provider internal management layers this agreed SLA need to be translated to objectives on the respective layers. The formulation of these objectives depend on the technology used and might not go down to all layers. For example the local management components that ensure the proper operation of resources on the physical layer should not be affected of any agreed SLA as their goals do not change.

Considering this loosely coupled view of the service providers it is necessary to motivate that similar to the previous management layers a VO management layer is needed at all. As the agreed SLAs regulate the external quality of the services also no error messages/events are communicated but SLA violations (either from the consumer or provider). The role of the VO Management block is therefore to detect SLA violations and to take the appropriate decisions based on these violations. These decisions need then to be communicated to relevant members of the VO. Potential reactions on SLA violations include the communication to the service provider responsible for accounting that a violation occurred and the agreed price penalties should be applied or to replace a service provider with a new provider.

As outlined above it is assumed that a limited number of SLAs is provided within one Virtual Organisation. Similarly the potential actions applied in case of violations should be pre-determined and their number should be limited. Additionally many research projects propose to add the potential applied penalties as part of the SLAs (see for example [107]).

5.3 Key Building Blocks

As shown in chapter 4 a wide range of monitoring solutions exists mostly limited to the surveillance of low level hardware metrics or service availabilities and mostly relying on humans to perform appropriate counter measures. Additionally the approaches for integrating the information from different layers stop very often at the system layer. Clearly no tool is considering the management of potentially conflicting obligations towards several consumers for different Virtual Organisations. Additionally the integration of economic considerations using not only technical parameters for the prioritisation of scarce resources but associated risks (high penalty for violating an SLA, violation of an SLA for an important customer, decrease of the reputation, ...) are not part of any existing solution.

The proposed solution extends the supervision approach in GeneSyS by adding a hierarchy of management layers inspired by Policy Based Management Approaches responsible for the management of different aspects. The approach also go far beyond pure monitoring solutions such as realised by INCA [127], GridICE [14] or MIMO [99]. The hierarchy has been motivated by the fact that decisions based on SLAs or others economic parameters are in the time frame from minutes to days and decisions close to the managed entities can be taken independent from them most of the time and require significant faster decisions. As indicated in table 5.2 different approaches for making decisions are proposed for the different layers.

Management Layer	Realisation	Decision Time
Local	Hardcoded, table based, dependency driven	milliseconds to seconds
Provider Internal	Rule based, policy driven	seconds up to minutes

Chapter 5 Monitoring and Management Concepts

Management Layer	Realisation	Decision Time
Provider Boundary	Policy driven, Human interaction	Minutes to days
VO wide	Policy driven, Human interaction	Minutes to years

Table 5.2: Anticipated typical methods and corresponding decision times

It is not possible to compare the complete proposed solution to existing approaches as only partial solutions do exist. Instead in the following section the innovations per layer and patterns for realising the functionality are discussed.

Manageability Layer In this layer the existing tools provide almost all necessary functionality. In particular for the realisation of the *Raw Data Sensor* component a wide range of possibilities exist. For the realisation of the *Resource Delegate* the choice of existing solution is less extensive but available. Additional more or less all tools allow the realisation of extensions (e.g. NAGIOS [110], Lemon [13], ...) that allow the addition of custom sensor types and data providers. Within the GeneSyS project the author and others have realised *Data Aggregation & Integration* and *Command Enforcement* components for different scenarios. This implementations had been also submitted to the OASIS standardisation group working on the Management Using Web Services (MUWS) specifications. Also the work of the Distributed Management Task Force (DMTF) with Web Based Enterprise Management (WBEM) and the Component Information Model (CIM) information model is in line with the proposed approach. Additionally further specialised information models such as the Grid Laboratory Uniform Environment (GLUE) [93] schema for High Performance Computing scenarios exist.

Additionally to the widely used pattern to add different kind of sensors to the monitored entities the innovation as presented by the author and others in [30, 32, 33, 34, 31] is to add the concept of *Resource Delegates* and to introduce the notion of self-monitoring of the system based on heartbeat messages. In [13] a similar approach using so called Fault Tolerance Actuators launched on the monitored entity in case of failures for performing counter measures is described.

Local Management Layer As most of the existing solutions are focused solely on the monitoring aspect no direct corresponding functionality can be found. Only the Fault Detection and

Recovery (FDR) concept integrated with the Lemon framework [13] realises something in this direction. The realised solution is called a fabric management framework that is able to handle hardware failures autonomously based on pre-defined fixed rules. However the proposed system does not consider a management hierarchy and no dynamic update of the rule sets.

The three major elements of a management block have been already described above in section 5.2.2. In this section the concept is further detailed. The first element is the *Data Receiver* receiving the data from the lower layers and apply some initial categorization on the data and evaluate the situation up the point where a decision is necessary. The *Command Sender* communicates the necessary commands in order to implement a decision. The *Enactor* component taking the decisions and is relying on the categorization done by the *Data Receiver* and utilizes the functionality for sending the decisions taken in a reliable way offered by the *Command Sender*. Figure 5.5 provide more details on a potential realisation of such a management block considering also the requirement that is must be 'stackable' and integrated into an overall management block hierarchy.

In the figure two communication flows are shown. The communication (indicated with the dotted and orange arrows) between different components and the potentially external repository containing the rules, policies or other data building the basis for the categorization and decisions. The solid and blue arrows show the communication within and outside a management block. The arrows are not numbered as all these communications can happen in parallel. In the *Data/Event Receiver* component one can see the *Message Cache* as the entry point for all information that is arriving from the manageability layer or lower management blocks. The *Categorization & Evaluation* component is pulling one or more messages at a time from the cache considering their priority and correlation. The messages are analysed and an initial evaluation is done (e.g. compare the values to be in or outside given boundaries). The evaluation result triggers a decision request towards the *Enactor* components. Again to unblock the operation the communication is not directly or blocking but via another cache called *Decision Queue*. The decision request is pulled out by the *Decision* module of the *Enactor* again using the information and knowledge stored in the rules/policy repository. The decision is pushed back into the *Decision Queue*. The decision is pulled out from the *Command Sender* that need to map the decision into a set of concrete commands. These commands need to be transmitted to the lower layers for their implementation in a reliable way. If a measure cannot be applied in the given timeframe a corresponding *Report Message* is generated and pushed into the *Message Queue* similar to external messages.

Additionally to this main data flow also external commands can be received from a higher layer management block (or a human operator). These commands are handled by the *Command Receiver*. This component either pushes the decision straight into the *Decision Queue* or to the *Deci-*

Chapter 5 Monitoring and Management Concepts

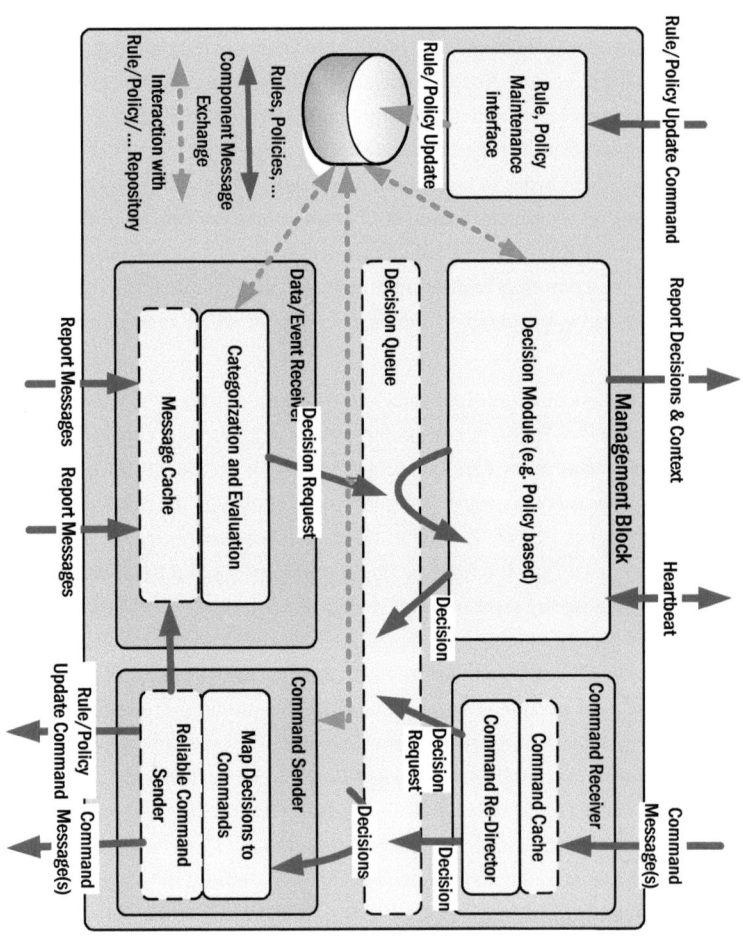

Figure 5.5: Concept for the realisation of all management blocks in the hierarchy

sion Module if a mapping from the decision to a set of decisions is necessary. Another possibility to influence the operation of the management block is via an update of the rule/policy repository. This update is again either requested by a human operator or other management blocks. It is quite obvious that the acceptance of commands for both cases would need to by accompanied by the appropriate security credentials that authorize the sender of the commands to perform these actions.

Intermediate Management Layer Some existing solutions consider already a hierarchy of management layers. For example the INCA [127] framework foresees a local management and a central monitoring component. The approach to have a local layer combined with a centralized component covering the complete VO is quite typical. The solution proposed here consider a potentially unlimited number of management layers where a number of four to five layers is seen as sensible number (see also chapter 6 for an example). This means that a management block needs to be 'stackable'. In figure 5.6 this interrelation is shown exemplarily with two layers. In this figure also the two orthogonal approaches for influencing the behaviour of lower management layers via commands is shown again. The first possibility is to send an 'Command' Message containing one ore more commands to be implemented (as shown in the last section to the *Command Receiver*). This message could be in response to a reported decision or could be driven by the policies/rules or the result of an 'Command' Message received from another layer above. The second approach proposed is that higher layers can update and modify the underlying rule or policy base. For example based on the good results with a low level of hardware degradation experienced with a certain type of hardware (analysed on a higher management layer) with a low number of reported errors the time interval for in-depth tests is increased. This change would be implemented by changing the corresponding rule on the lower layer.

As discussed already above while the concept is hierarchical each of the layers are still acting autonomously. So considering the case that the communication between the layers is broken the lower layer still is able to take management decision. Obviously no rule or policies update can take place so the decision basis will not change and adapt and no commands will arrive. If the communication is operational again depending on the time elapsed the commands and updates will be transmitted with a delay utilizing the reliable sending mechanism. Additionally the management blocks will be aware of the problem due to their self-monitoring capabilities as indicated by the heartbeat message exchange.

Provider Boundary Management Layer The assumption taken so far is that the message flow between the different management blocks is only controlled by security policies and the ap-

Chapter 5 Monitoring and Management Concepts

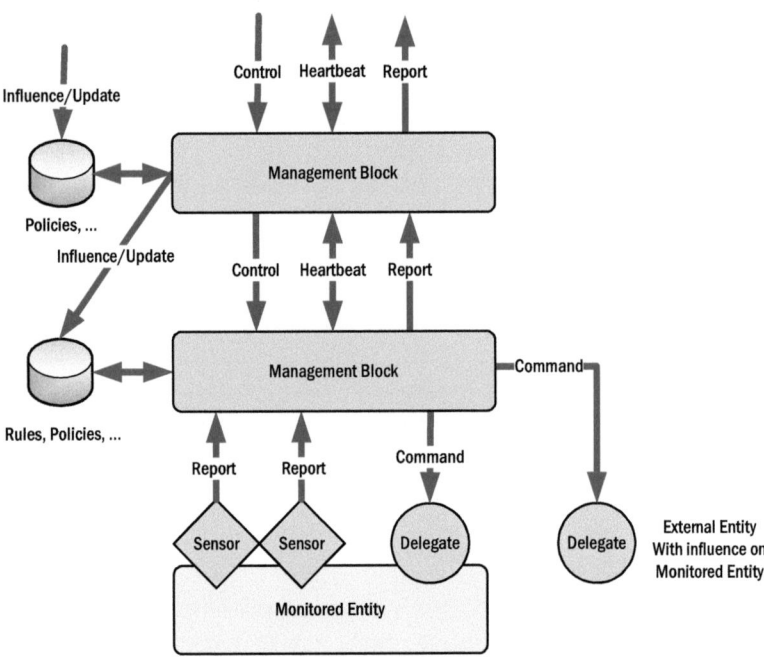

Figure 5.6: Chaining concept for the internal management

5.3 Key Building Blocks

proach to data confidentiality is limited to a potential encryption of the communication channel. However as discussed already above in section 5.2.2 at the boundary of the service provider a more complex control infrastructure is needed. The reason for this is the assumed autonomous behaviour of the service providers. The autonomy in such a strict sense as considered here where a provision of detailed information about the status towards the VO is seen as clear non-goal and the relationship is fully based on external SLAs it is not surprising that none of the existing deployments of computational Grids have something similar in their architecture. A cross-provider scenario is not part of the specification of scenarios anticipated for Web Based Enterprise Management (WBEM) and consequently no considerations along this line has been influencing their architecture.

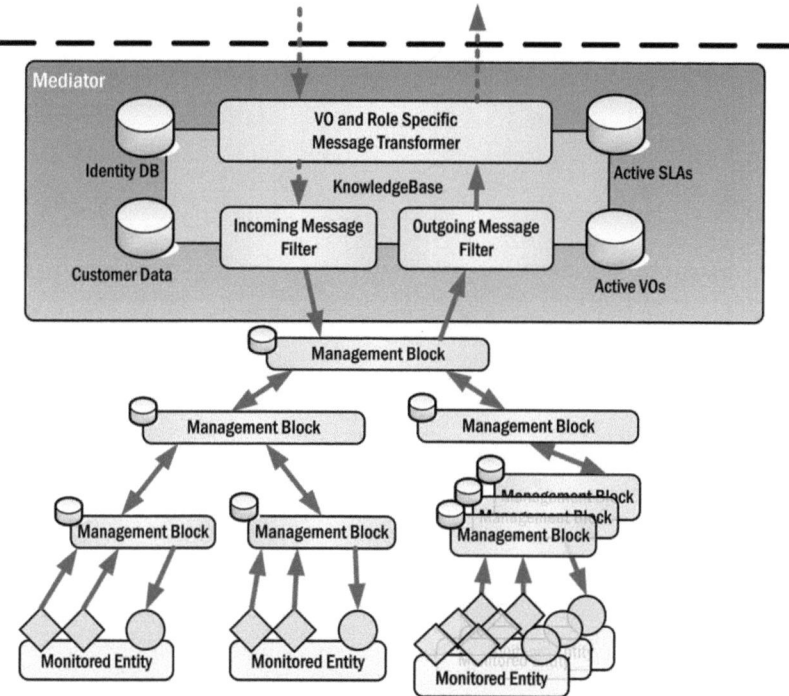

Figure 5.7: boundary management

Additionally the implementation of the *Mediator* component is quite dependant from the concrete scenario. In figure 5.7 the specific nature of the filter components and the message trans-

Chapter 5 Monitoring and Management Concepts

formation has been simply indicated by the knowledge base underpinning them. This knowledge base combining information on security (identity database), existing customer data (e.g. how important is this customer?) with currently running SLAs und active VOs of the provider.

VO Management Layer The role of the VO Management layer depends on the underlying organisational model. For this thesis as defined in chapter 2 the assumption is that all relationships between the different providers are safeguarded by SLAs. This means that in the first place no VO wide management entity would be needed. If there is no dominant partner within the virtual organisation as in the hub-and-spoke topology (see section 2.3.1.1) or one of the partner is accepted as a Trusted Third Party (TTP) there is a need for an independent entity that is storing agreed SLAs, is monitoring the implementation of the agreed SLAs and is potentially acting as a clearing house in case of violation and disagreements.

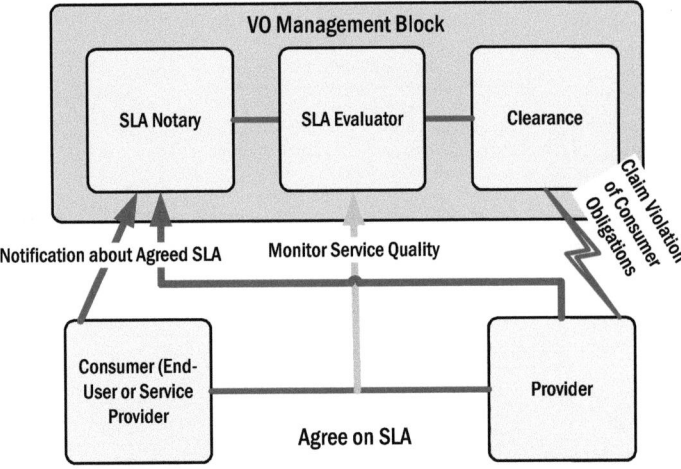

Figure 5.8: VO Management block

As shown in figure 5.8 the VO management block is divided into three major blocks (1) the SLA notary, (2) the SLA Evaluator and (3) the Clearance component. The role of the first block is simply to store the mutually signed and agreed SLAs either negotiated on the fly using an SLA negotiation protocol or agreed out of band. The second component requires a mechanism allowing to measure if the obligations agreed within an SLA have been met. This implies that the agreed SLAs can be either measured from the outside or both consumer and provider agrees to an instrumentation by the TTP acting as the VO manager allowing to measure within the domains. In case of a SLA violation and a disagreement between consumer and provider a notification about the conflict is issued towards the clearance component. This component uses the stored SLAs and the collected information from the SLA Evaluator in order to take a decision.

Chapter 6

Application of the Concept

The management concept presented in the last chapter needs further detailing before it can be applied to a concrete case. The concept does neither imply a certain number of layers nor does it detail the interaction process between the different components within the management blocks.

In this chapter such a detailed design for the service provider management is done for an HPC utility provider offering computational services via Grid middleware. It is assumed that the services are offered based on Service Level Agreements.

6.1 HPC computing utility provider

This provider is specialised in the delivery of services closely related to the operation of high end physical resources for computing and data storage. The following services are supposed to be delivered via standardized interfaces and controlled by agreed Service Level Agreements.

- Submission of jobs, monitoring of their progress and basic control over the job such as cancel the operation
- Storage of input data, staging of data and storage of result data
- Remote access to intermediate and final result data

In order to have the possibility to discuss certain management policies or rules in the necessary detail it is further assumed that the provider is providing access to the systems via Secure Shell (SSH) and using the Grid middleware *Uniform Access over the Internet to Computing Resources (UNICORE)* (see section 4.1.2.1). A Unified Modeling Language deployment view of the considered case is shown in figure 6.1.

Chapter 6 Application of the Concept

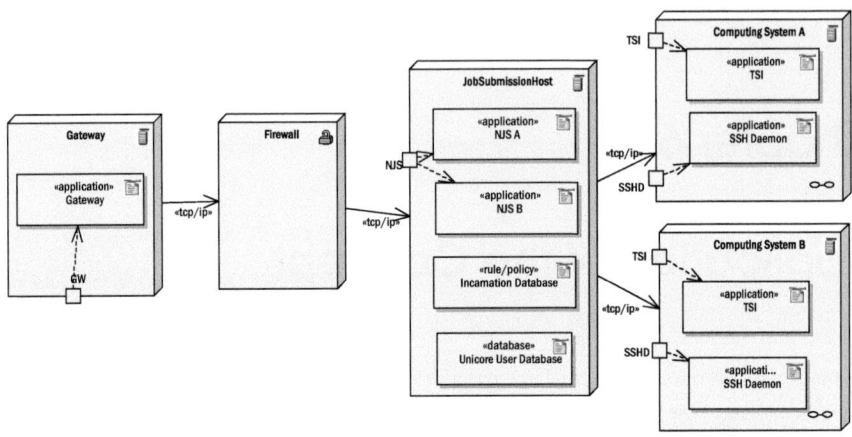

Figure 6.1: Deployment view of the services for the HPC utility provider

The management tasks for this provider are distributed across the following three layers (1) Business Relation Management Layer, (2) Resource Management Layer and (3) tree type of Local Management layers. The first layer is responsible to manage the business relations expressed on one hand via agreed Service Level Agreements and on the other hand by existing customer relations expressed in Customer Relationship Management (CRM) databases, Project, User & Accounting Databases or any other kind of system where an identity is mapped to the type of customer. This layer is motivated as a mapping from these externally agreed constraints has to be done in order to allow the more resource oriented layers to perform appropriate. The customer information is in particular relevant as on one hand the agreed SLAs might reference to existing *non-electronic* contracts that influence additionally the operation modalities. In particular in situations where the demand is higher then the availability of resources and a prioritisation of the SLAs need to be done customer relations need to be balanced against the associated risk violating a particular SLA. So it might be better not to violate an SLA with a penalty of 1.000 € of an *important* customer and to risk a penalty of 10.000 € associated with another SLA. This might be the right decision as violating an SLA influence the reputation of a provider and going below a certain threshold might have impact on expected future business relations.

The next layer between the local management layers and this economically oriented layer is on one hand in charge of the mediation between these two extremes but is also necessary to allow

6.1 HPC computing utility provider

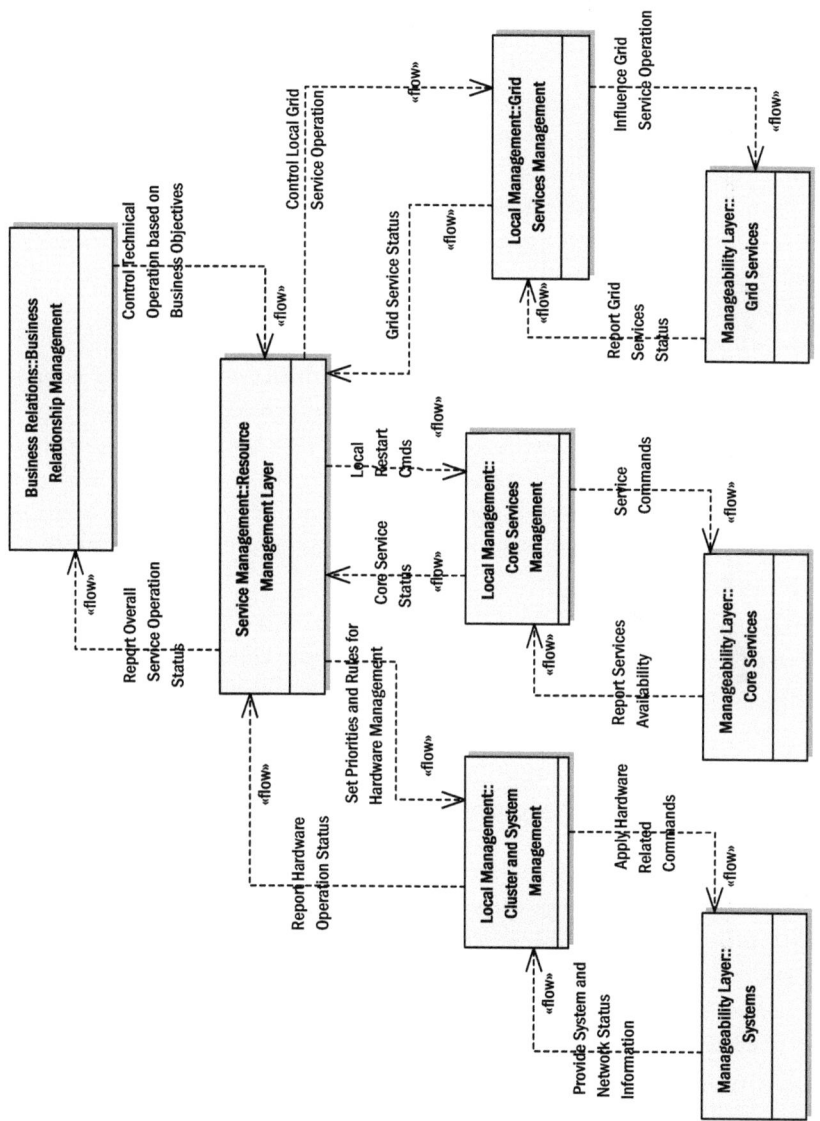

Figure 6.2: Chosen layers and their relations

Chapter 6 Application of the Concept

the local management layers to be really specialised and consequently fast. So the integration task to deliver a complete viewpoint from all the different pieces necessary to deliver a certain service is performed on this layer.

The lowest layers have been divided for the considered case into three categories. The first layer is responsible for the management of the compute clusters and other server components hosting e.g. the Grid middleware components. Additionally the network management is allocated on this layer. The management of the core services for the remote access such as SSH daemons or the regular execution of tools to detect the system health from a software viewpoint are controlled by the core service management layer. The Grid components (in this case UNICORE) such as the Network Job Supervisor (NJS) or Target System Interface (TSI) are managed by the Grid services management layer. While at a first glance this looks quite similar to the core services monitoring the major deviation is related to the possibilities related to the active influencing of the operation of the services. An SSH daemon allows only a kind of binary operation such as block access for a certain user or IP address a Grid middleware system allow more fine grained, more complex possibilities to influence the operation. For example the Incarnation Database (IDB) transformation rules for a generic Abstract Job Object into site and machine specific values could be changed to map *high priority* to different queues on the target system or where the externally usable application *foo* is located.

Below these three management layers for each local management system there is a manageability layer that is providing in compliance with the model proposed in the previous chapter independent from the underlying monitoring tool the monitoring information and potential monitoring errors in an at least provider wide standardized format.

6.1.1 Realising the Manageability Layer

The realisation of the information gathering can rely on a wide range of existing tools. The concrete selection of the tools is mostly dependent on the monitored resource. For smaller cluster systems GANGLIA [12] or for large systems Lemon [13] or Nagios [110] might be used. For network monitoring the Simple Network Management Protocol (SNMP) [128] protocol or proprietary sensors are possible. There is no need to implement any additional tool or protocol to realise the metering and instrumentation layer.

However as discussed before the availability of all these individual data is not sufficient in order to derive a complete picture of the overall system state. Additionally for the further processing of the monitored data the steps of aggregation and integration need to be performed and the data need to be transformed to a standardized format. These steps are shown in the format of an UML

6.1 HPC computing utility provider

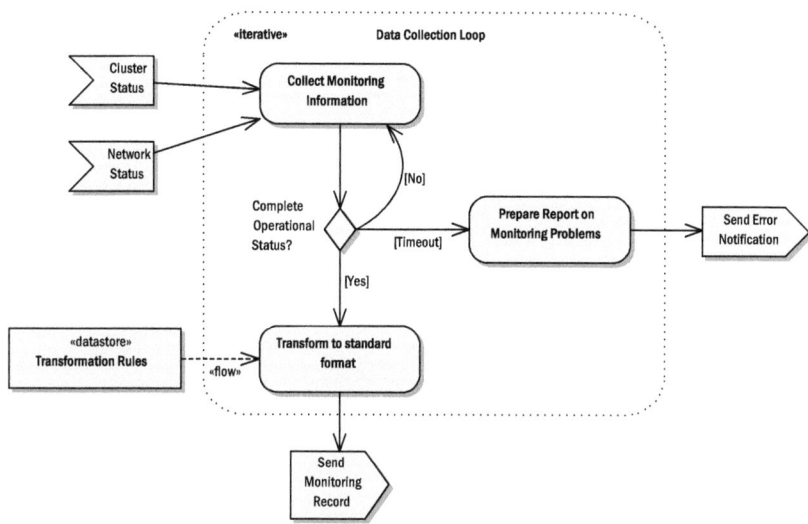

Figure 6.3: Data collection for the System and Network Layer

Activity Diagram in figure 6.3 for the example of the hardware and network monitoring. The data provided for example by the above mentioned tools are shown as input events and received by a data collector aiming to consolidate all this information to *monitoring records* summarizing a complete status. If a record can be completed it is handed over to the transformation activity producing from the internal data structure a message e.g. in XML format. If a record cannot be completed in a pre-defined period in time a monitoring error message is produced.

While the process in the figure is focused on the system and management data monitoring for the other two manageability layers the process is similar. In the implementation of this approach in the Generic System Supervision (GeneSyS) project the components performing this operations hadn't been placed on the monitored entity or system but on a dedicated resource within the same physical network.

6.1.2 Local Management

In section 5.2.2 and 5.3 a quite complex management block had been introduced realised with decoupled components for receiving the data and events, taking decisions on what to do with the data and a separate block for the reliable delivery of taken decisions and corresponding com-

Chapter 6 Application of the Concept

mands. The overhead introduced by such a decoupled realisation must not be in the same order of the requested decision times expected by the respective layer. For the local management where decisions are taken in seconds such a complex realisation is not the appropriate solution.

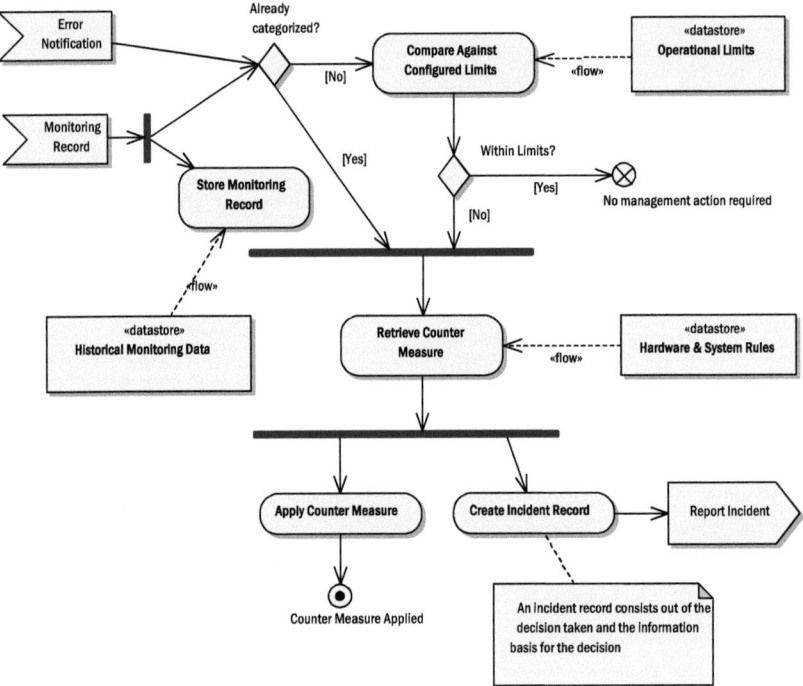

Figure 6.4: Activities for the Local System and Network Management

In figure 6.4, again for the system and network management domain, the necessary activity flow is shown. All components of the management block are in this case realised without any intermediate queues. The first step is to perform an assessment of the received messages and compare them against defined limits for operation. In case the retrieved message is an error or has been assessed to be out of the given limits the defined counter measure is retrieved from the rules datastore. The counter measure is applied in parallel to the incident report created for the Resource Management Layer.

Similar to the manageability layer there is no significant difference between these system and network case and the other domains core services and Grid components in this process. The differ-

6.1 HPC computing utility provider

ence would be in the two datastores for the operational limits and the rules of the counter measures. For the system monitoring messages like lack of free disk space or disk failures would be reported leading to counter measures such as scheduling repair or in-depth checks for the disks. For the core services the reported problems could be lack of response from a daemon process (e.g. sshd) and the initiation of a restart attempt.

It is important to keep these rules simple in order to allow the anticipated fast response. The more complex analysis of the problem situation is performed on the higher layers where also the received errors are correlated. Another reason to keep these rules simple is that complex rules increase the risk of unplanned interference of different measures. As the quality of the management depends directly on the quality of the rules, it is expected that the rules are defined by system administrators with the appropriate knowledge how to cope with certain situations. Additionally to this direct update from human operators the hierarchical management concepts foresees also the possibility that these rules are updated e.g. in response to reported incidents.

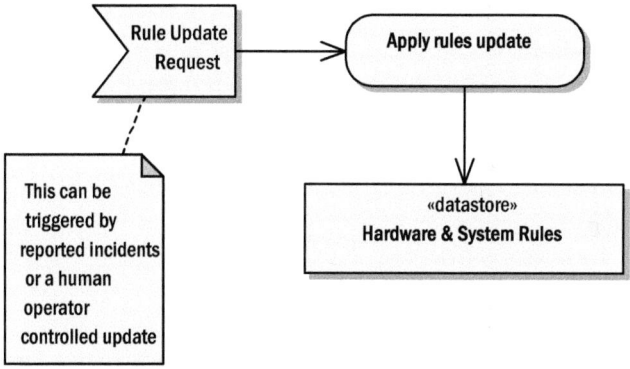

Figure 6.5: Update of the Rules Datastore

The update procedure (see figure 6.5) is also started by an event that could be a message retrieved by the management block. This message could be created from an end-user application for system administrators supporting the rule definition or could be the activation of a pre-defined rule based on the previously reported incidents. If several recovery mechanisms for the UNICORE Target System Interface (TSI) has been performed by applying the rule `Restart TSI` without success some action is needed on the higher layers (e.g. removing the system from the available Grid systems) but a new rule on the system level saying that the node should be put into maintenance mode making an in-depth testing and a complete system reboot instead of continue to try to restart the TSI is needed as well. While in some cases a real update of the rule (e.g. by replacing the corresponding XML file) is performed there is also the possibility to change the default rule activating a new measure. Such a rule change is clearly preferable from a security viewpoint as not the contents of the rules can be changed but only if they are active or not.

6.1.3 Service Management

With the availability of the local management layers an optimised operation oriented on *technical* parameters can be already realised in a quite efficient way. The structure of the local management has been chosen to be specialised in order to realise a short response time on failures and problems. This specialisation comes with the drawback that the applied measures are based on limited information within the associated monitoring domain and no coordination of the layers exists. While in the example an integration of information about the different parts of a cluster (CPU, Memory, Disk, Interconnect, temperature, ...) is done having a complete status from the hardware viewpoint on the cluster system.

The service management layer is addressing this problem by integrating these individual views to a complete picture of all resources and core services needed in order to deliver services to external consumers. The service management layer is implementing the full management block components as shown in figure 5.5 in the previous chapter as the decision process is anticipated to be more complex and consequently slower. So the overhead in time introduced with the decoupling is acceptable compared to the decision time.

6.1.3.1 Report Categorization and Evaluation

At this level in the hierarchy the information flood from the sensors at the various levels have been already aggregated on the manageability layers. The local management layer has further reduced the amount of information by performing a comparison with defined normal operation conditions generating potentially *Incident Reports*. These reports are received by the service management layer for further processing. Figure 6.6 shows the design for the *DataReceiver* part of the overall management block. The received report is stored in an incoming message queue. From this queue reports are pulled out regularly and if not already pre-assigned with a category indicating immediate decisions the report is categorized and evaluated. The categorization is based on the information stored in the *Knowledge Base (KB)*. The knowledge base consists out of different type of information responsible for different parts of the categorization. For example the KB could contain simple rules assigning an urgency category to different type of reports calculating the priority based on the type of the report (failure, maintenance required, warning, regular sta-

6.1 HPC computing utility provider

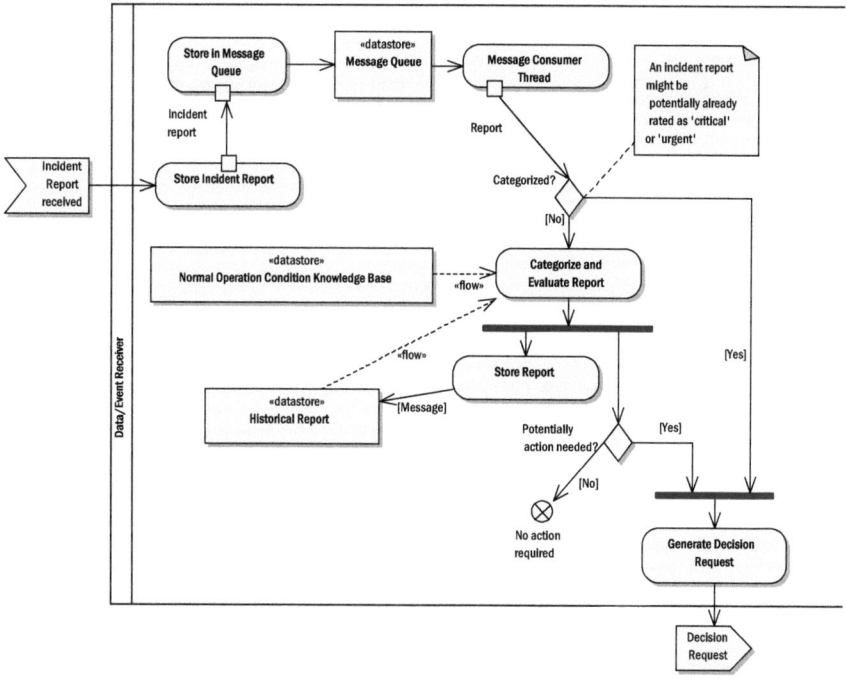

Figure 6.6: DataReceiver component for the Service Management Layer

Chapter 6 Application of the Concept

tus) increasing the priority one level for each report of the same type received within a given time frame. Beside the urgency other priorities such as importance or associated impact might be assigned based on the information in the KB. As described in section 4.3 several approaches exists for performing such a categorization. If infrastructure information is available several reports can be related. For this correlation the information in the historical report datastore but also the message queue with their pending reports is the information basis for detecting potentially related reports. Based on this process the Report is amended with the retrieved knowledge and stored in the Historical report database. In parallel a *Decision Request* is generated and pushed towards the Decision queue.

For the case considered in this chapter many potential interdependencies across the management domains do exist. The core services depend on the proper operation of the underlying hardware. A failure report for the *sshd* would be related to corresponding failure reports from the hardware and network layer. The Grid middleware relies not only on the hardware hosting the Grid services themselves but also on the core services (e.g. a functioning perl system for running the TSI script), the operation of the queuing system, etc. These relations are assumed to be infrequently changing and therefore externally modelled (see also section 6.2).

6.1.3.2 Decision Module

This module operates quite similar to the Policy Decision Point (PDP) of the Policy based Management concept. Based on the prepared information of the *DataReceiver* component now a decision about potential counter measures can be taken. The general activity flow shown in figure 6.7 does not imply a certain method to derive the decision. As an dependency analysis (based on external knowledge e.g. modelled by a human operator) has been performed the initial step is now to aim to classify the incidents to be of 'primary' or 'secondary' nature. Secondary incidents will not appear again if the problems leading to one or more primary incidents are resolved. Such a classification is not seen as essential for making a decision but would increase the probability to find the best solution as the measures could concentrate on a lower number of incidents. If on this level no decision can be taken how to solve the experienced problems it must be immediately escalated to a higher management layer. If a decision could be taken it is stored in the *Decision Queue* for further processing by the *CommandSender* component. Additionally the taken decision together with the incidents is reported to the higher layer.

For the considered HPC utility provider scenario a complete system failure or the failure of a critical resource without a replacement possibility would by the case for the escalation procedure to the higher layers as this would have clearly impact on the business layer (likely leading to violation

6.1 HPC computing utility provider

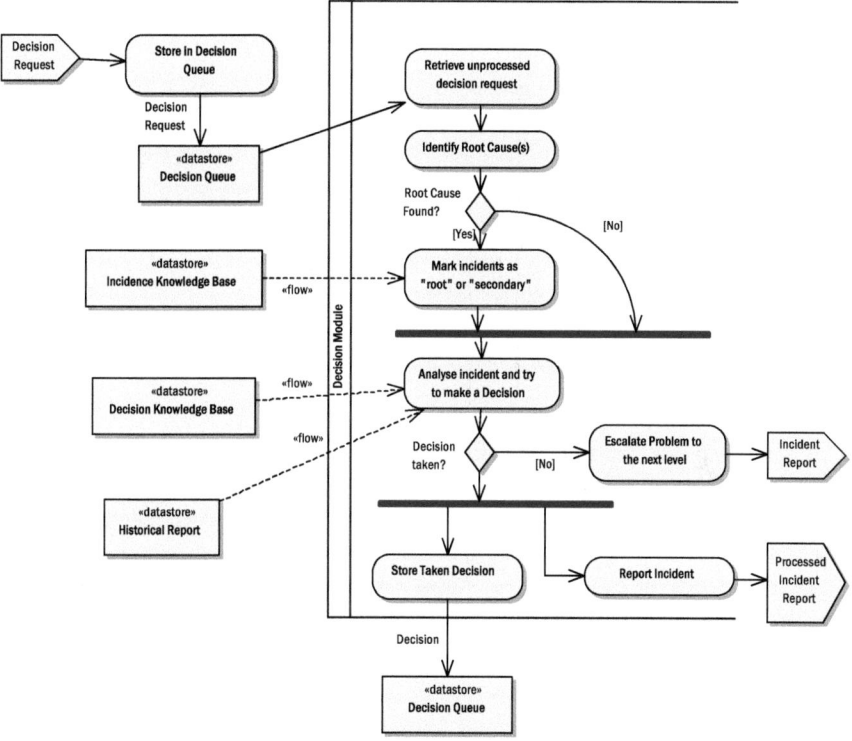

Figure 6.7: Activity flow for the decision process

Chapter 6 Application of the Concept

of SLAs).

This layer in between the business and resource oriented management layers is also responsible to realise the mapping between these two viewpoints. In this role the decision knowledge base is assumed to contain the technical boundary conditions for the business level SLAs from the higher layer. An incident report might indicate an error (as in the example above of the underlying hardware system) but more frequently it is expected that the incidents report an operation close to the given limits or outside the pre-defined limits. So on this layer this is assessed based on the decision knowledge base if the parameter boundaries for the whole system are still met or if additional resources are necessary. Such additional resources could be granting more CPU and memory to a XEN instance hosting an NJS but also assuming a dynamically partitioned cluster system on the computational part. So if the current operational status (reported by the Local Management Layer via the Incident reports) indicates a potential violation of the given technical boundaries stored in the knowledge base of the overall system corrective measure would be taken. For example if jobs submitted via the Grid middleware are supposed to be prioritized against jobs issued via other means and the reported average waiting time for Grid jobs submitted are above the threshold (an therefore triggered the creation of incident reports) a potential decision taken on this level would be to implement a further prioritisation of the Grid submitted jobs.

6.1.3.3 Mapping Decisions to Commands

The first step for solving a problem is to analyse it (*DataReceiver* component), the next step is to take a decision and now the decision need to be translated into concrete actions to be done. In the last example the decision was taken to prioritize Grid jobs against non-Grid jobs. There is now a range of measures that could be applied to implement these decisions. On the resource level one could solve it by dedicating compute nodes to Grid jobs, limit the allowed job size for non-Grid jobs or change the mapping of the priorities expressed in the Abstract Job Object to job queues by changing the entries in the Incarnation Database of the UNICORE system. The activity flow proposed in 6.8 proposes to differentiate the cases where a measure can be applied expecting a short term solution and where the improvement of the situation is not expected to realise shortly. In the latter case the rules on the lower layers triggering the secondary incident reports are updated on one hand to stop reporting the problem but at the same time a rule that is triggered if the effect of the counter measure has been realised to restore the previous situation is added. A realisation of such behaviour could be realised by supporting a 'disable rule' command for the rule/policy databases and the corresponding 'enable rule'. Beside these secondary activities the commands necessary to implement the decision need to be derived and finally but into the sending loop de-

6.1 HPC computing utility provider

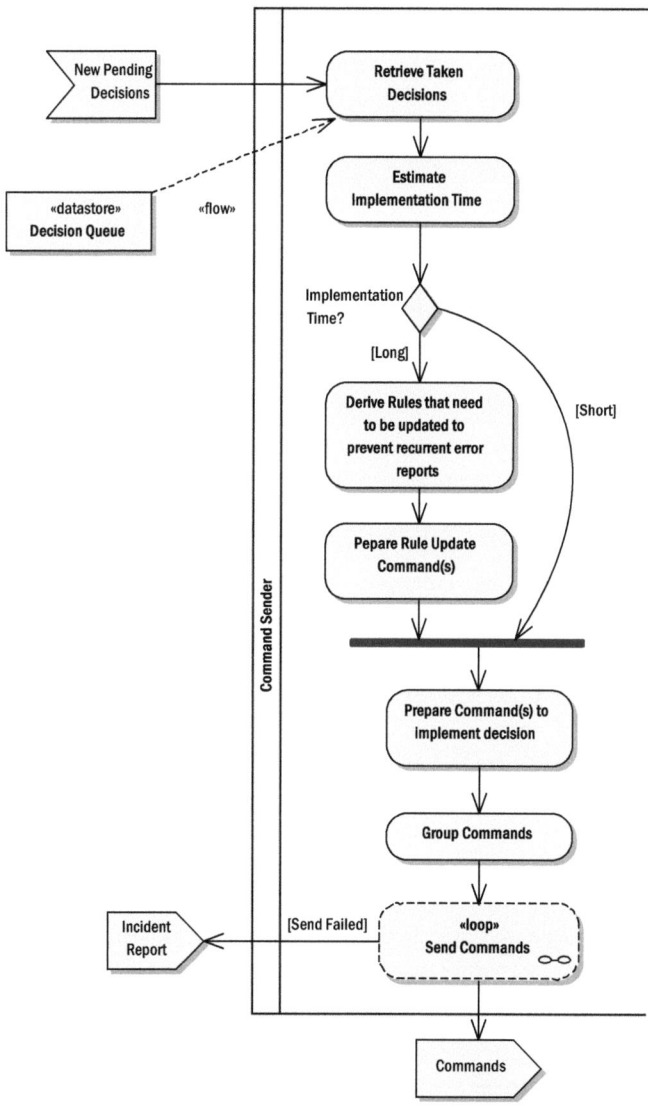

Figure 6.8: Activity flow for reliable command sending

livering the commands to the corresponding lower layers. If commands need to be implemented in a certain order the *Send Commands* loop is considering this order decided during the command preparation activities before.

6.1.3.4 Rule updates and Command Reception

The management block concepts foresees two additional blocks. Both blocks are accepting commands from a higher management layer. The first one accept commands leading to an update of the Rule/Policy datastores and the other one receives commands to be implemented by concrete set of actions (including rule/policy updates on lower layers).

On the Service management layer the commands will come from the business relations layer and are supposed to influence the technical operations driven by business objectives. So the rule/policy updates are based on newly agreed SLAs, change of priority of a customer or other aspects covered on the business relations layer. Additionally other commands might be send to this layer that need to be mapped to *Decisions* in order to push them similar to locally taken *Decisions* in the *Decision Queue* for further processing. For the considered HPC scenario this could be a command to prioritize a certain user group (e.g. as they have an external demonstration) for a certain time period. This command would need to be mapped as any internal decision down to a set of commands influencing the mapping of priorities in the Grid middleware or opening access to certain job submission queues or similar. All these operations might trigger additional action on the service management layer. For example an update of the knowledge base trigger also a notification towards the Decisor as depending on the significance of the change further actions might be necessary.

Additionally to this event driven actions a *Decision Request* can also be triggered by regular messages that are put into the *DecisionQueue* if a certain time period has elapsed. An example for the service management layer would be a regular maintenance procedure. This procedure would lead to a notification to the higher layers reporting the decision that now a certain group of resources will be put out of production for a maintenance cycle and to commands on the lower layer to actually perform the maintenance activities such as the launch of performance and degradation tests or reboot operations.

6.1.4 Business Relations

The management layer described in the previous section was still driven by technical constraints and did not interface with external information sources relevant for the operation of the overall service provider infrastructure. On the business relation layer the non-technical aspects are the pre-dominant factors. As this layer is on top of the management hierarchy the understanding that business objectives are the driving and controlling aspects of the overall management solutions are clearly expressed.

In this layer the currently active Service Level Agreements and also the information about the customers associated with these SLAs are the major source of information for the management decisions based on the reported incidents about the infrastructure situation within the service provider domain. A limitation already considered for the management concept and similarly for the HPC scenario is that the number of provided SLAs must be small. This means that still SLAs can be dynamically negotiated between service consumers and the service providers, but not in a complete free way. The negiotiation would be then reduced to selecting an SLA out of the offered ones. This is necessary as the mapping from a business level SLA to a technical level SLA expressed in concrete demands on the underlying infrastructure can only be defined in advance.

In table 6.1 the considered SLAs for the HPC utility scenario are shown together with their potential impact on the lower layers. The SLAs are described here in a quite informal way to motivate them rather then in a formal description using for example the XML based Web Service Level Agreement (WSLA) or WS-Agreement [129] formats.

Name	Description	Impact
Guaranteed Environment	This SLA ensures the provision of a certain environment for the end-user. This covers all aspects from a specific computer architecture, versions of specific applications and tools, minimum disk space, environment variables etc.	The impact of this SLA is that while SLAs of this type are active no change in the underlying infrastructure can be made. Services bound to this SLA cannot be easily moved to other compute environments. An easy way to guarantee such an environment is using virtualization techniques or if this is not possible to offer only the pre-defined standard configuration of a system.

Name	Description	Impact
Prioritized Access	In Addition to the guaranteed environment this SLA ensures a prioritized treatment. The prioritization does not guarantee a certain time when a job is started or a guaranteed time for the completion. The prioritization is relative to other jobs only. These kind of SLAs are often referred as 'soft' guarantees.	If no provider wide scheduling system is in place the prioritization can be done on the level of the Grid middleware where priorities are mapped on certain queues on the local scheduling system and by granting access to prioritized queues only to certain users.
Timed Access	As a further extension of the prioritized access only delivering a soft guarantee this SLA would guarantee a resource at a certain point in time e.g. for realising interactive access or application steering scenarios.	The support of SLAs of this type require a special support from the underlying queuing system.
Exclusive Access	This SLA guarantees not only a predefined environment but ensures that the whole compute system is available for an exclusive utilization and the access is granted with the highest priority. This SLA is seen as beneficial for users that cannot allow other jobs within the same compute system for confidentiality reasons.	The easiest way to support such an SLA would be a resource that is fully provided in an exclusive mode to a specific customer. As this might lead to quite long idle times of the resource an operation dropping immediately running low priority jobs if a job bound to this Exclusive Access SLA is started.

Table 6.1: SLAs for the HPC utility provider case

Even if the SLAs in the table above would have been described in an XML based format their realisation on the service management layer cannot be done by just applying an appropriate transformation rule. The challenge is that multiple SLAs at once for different customers and for different potentially competing VOs need to be implemented. For this reason a more complex process for deriving the necessary updates of the rules on the service management layer is necessary. As the

6.1 HPC computing utility provider

general structure of the *DataReceiver, Decisor* and *CommandSender* blocks are similar to the one on the service management layer the flow shown in figure 6.9 focuses on the logical flow and do not repeat again the queues and processes for storing and pushing the different types of messages. The process shown in figure 6.9 is triggered by the availability of a newly agreed SLA. It does not

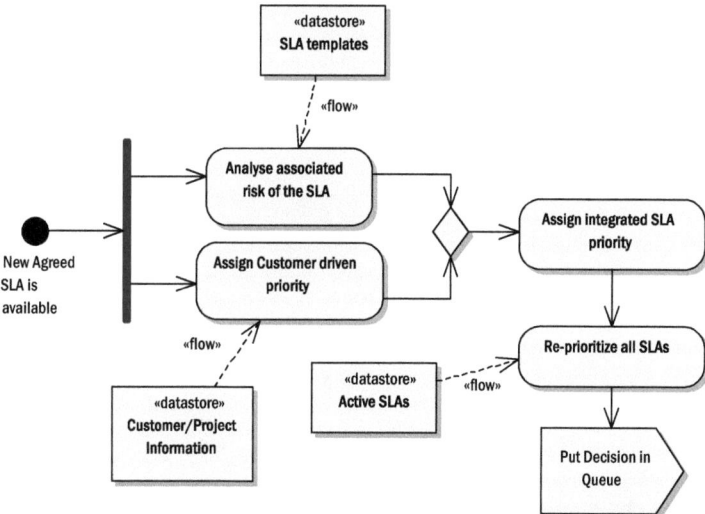

Figure 6.9: Activity flow triggered by the availability of a new SLA

matter if this agreement has been reached using an electronic negotiation protocol or is based on a regular contract. The contract indicates between whom the contract has been established, the agreed obligations to be met (as shown in the table above) by consumer and provider and potentially also the penalties applied in case of SLA violations. The process to decide on the priority of the SLA compared to the other currently active SLAs is based on the type of the SLA and its associated risk to implement it and depends for whom this SLA is offered. SLAs of important customers might be treated with higher priority compared to others as the potential risk cannot be limited to one single SLA but all SLAs of the same customer or anticipated future collaborations need to be considered. If a decision about the priority of the SLA have been reached combining both viewpoints the SLA need to be added at the corresponding place in the list of currently active SLAs triggering a change in priority of all SLAs below the new SLA.

Such a re-assessment would also be necessary if updates of the knowledge bases are happening based on an update of the customer properties or an updated view on the risk of failure for an SLA.

Additionally if an active SLA is terminated or the service management layer reports failures and problems and potentially some active SLAs need to be completely neglected in order to safeguard other SLAs. All these decisions to re-prioritize or even completely drop the operation for certain SLAs requires the communication of the decision in the form of commands to the lower layers. Based on the assumption that the number of SLAs is limited these mapping rules are assumed to be pre-defined for different priority classes as discussed above defined by the SLA itself but also by the customer that have co-signed the agreement.

6.1.5 Mediation Component

The management concept proposes at the boundary of a service provider a component called *Mediator*. This component is intended to control the message flow between the provider and the outside world. For the HPC utility provider scenario no incoming message flow from the management viewpoint is foreseen. So the incoming message filter as shown in figure 5.7 would just block all incoming command messages. At the boundary of the service provider potentially a component negotiating SLAs with other providers or consumers is foreseen. This component delivers as incoming message the agreed SLAs to be implemented by the chain of management layers. In a similar way the only messages that pass the outgoing message filter and the transformation block translating the provider internal messages to a possibly different format used within the VO are SLA violation notifications.

6.2 Operational Considerations

The operation of the different management layers rely heavily on the knowledge, policy or rule bases driving the decisions. The maintenance of this datastores requires expert knowledge of the respective domain. So in order to set-up a management system based on the three layers proposed for the HPC utility provider case different actors can be identified that are necessary to operate the proposed system.

System Administrators are responsible for the instrumentation of the monitored resources, maintain the system rule datastore and also define several regular operational conditions. Additionally the System Administrator is contributing with knowledge about the dependency of resources.

Technical Policy Designers also defines rules and policies about the dependencies in order to feed the incidence knowledge base but additionally has to define the content of the decision knowledge base for the technical layer. This datastore must contain the policy obligations for reacting on the reported unresolved incidents from the local management layers but also covers operations with an impact on the business as on the local management layer such as regular maintenance procedures. The Technical Policy Designer also contributes to the definition of the mapping from business level SLAs to technical parameters.

Business Policy Managers are also contributing to the definition of the SLA mapping rules but mostly deal with the design and maintenance of offered SLAs in order to meet customer and market demands. As the customer relationships are also relevant for the mapping and prioritization process the Business Policy Manager need to define the rules how certain parameters such as *good* customer are defined and how they map to an increase in priority.

These roles together with the executed use cases as shown in figure 6.10 outline on a very high level the necessary tasks to operate the management infrastructure.

It is quite obvious that the maintenance of such databases are vital for the successful operation of the overall infrastructure and must be possible during the operation of the management framework. Beside these maintenance and knowledge engineering oriented tasks the actors on the different layers must be enabled to perform at least the activities expected to be covered in an automated way by the respective layers. So the System Administrator should be able to access the monitoring data in order to see the overall status of the different hardware and software resources and should be able to trigger counter measures in case the current situation is not covered by an existing rule and does not lead to an automated action by the *Decisor* component. The *Technical Policy Designer* should be similarly enabled to see an overall status of all local management layers, a list of reported incidents and the possible actions that can be taken ranging from response activities up to the regular maintenance activities out of the regular schedule. The *Business Policy Manager* should be able to change priorities of certain SLAs and in general able to influence the processes on the business relations layer. Of course the different roles can be performed by a single human person which makes in particular sense for the *System Administrator* and *Technical Policy Designer* roles.

Chapter 6 Application of the Concept

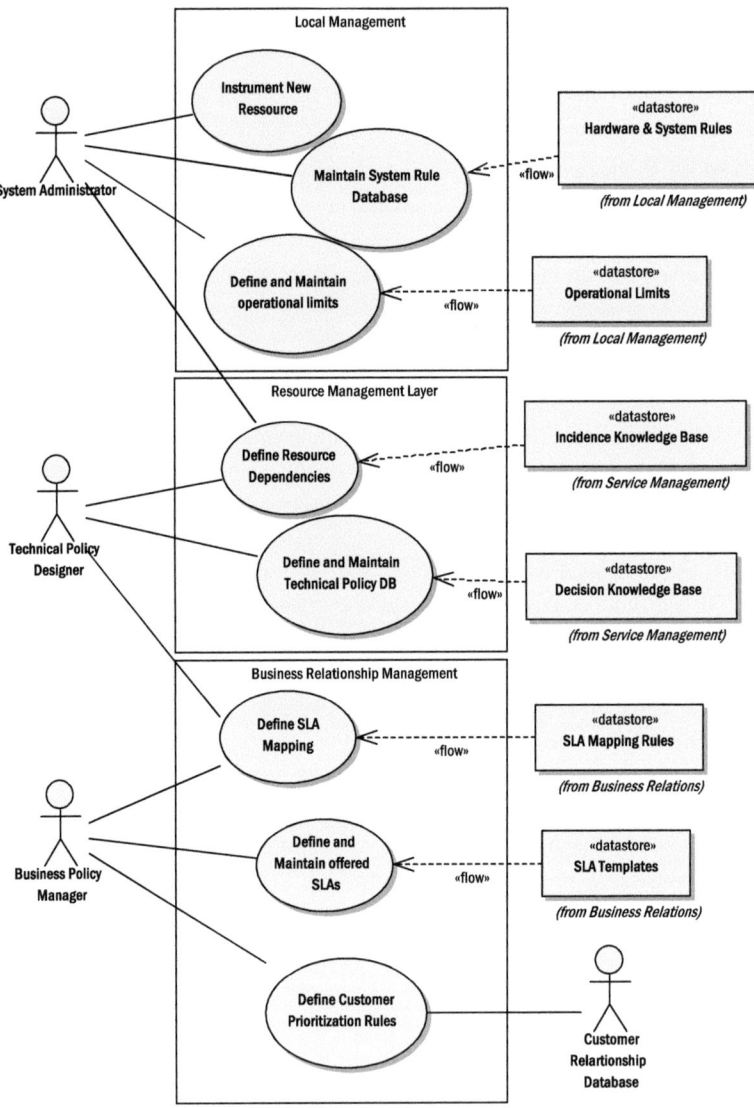

Figure 6.10: Roles and Use Cases

Chapter 7

Conclusion and Outlook

The current practice for controlling large scale distributed systems such as computational Grids is based on rather simple monitoring approaches that are only operational with the help of a comparably large number of human operators. Additionally the approach to ultimately collect the monitoring data at a central place often referred to as Grid Operations Centre (GOC) is not in line with the demands of a large set of applications where the collaboration is not based on common interests or a shared research vision but driven by economic factors. In such collaborations all relationships need to be safeguarded by Service Level Agreements. With this new model for Virtual Organisation inspired by the research results in the domain of Virtual Enterprises/Enterprise Networks also a new approach for ensuring the operation of the distributed application is needed.

In this thesis the proposed approach is based on several almost independently operating layers optimized for their domain exchanging in an asynchronous communication model from lower layers to the higher layers the detected problems and the locally applied solutions. The higher layers can potentially with their more global view come to a different conclusion and can overrule such decisions. The command chain from higher layers to lower layers can be either by direct commands to influence ultimately the underlying hardware and software infrastructure or by changing the knowledge bases of the management framework or the managed entities. This flow of reports and commands is mediated at the service provider level as another important aspect not reflected in existing deployments is the site autonomy in all internal management decisions. So at the boundary of the providers there is the need for controlling the information flow (e.g. about reported problems) or the acceptance from external commands.

In this way the management solution splits into three major parts. The highest level, the VO Management level, is dealing with the management of service providers applying penalties on SLA violations such as reduced payments up to the complete replacement of a provider. Within the service provider domain the management is typically realised using multiple layers. In the discussed ex-

Chapter 7 Conclusion and Outlook

ample three layers had been proposed dealing with hardware and low level services management, high level service management and the business management layer aiming to map business objectives to technical metrics. Additionally it might be necessary to have a light weighted consumer management. This assumption is driven by the assumption that SLA based relationships are not only applied between Service Providers but also between the consumer and the providers. This demands also a controlled behaviour on the client side.

The results of this work cannot be applied to existing eScience oriented infrastructures currently widely used by the particle physics community as the used VO model is conceptually different from the SLA driven model presented here. The gap between the existing eScience Grid deployments, the research work around SLA driven Virtual Organisations done within the Next Generation Grids research community where also this thesis fits in are currently only deployed with short duration within research project demonstrators or business experiments. For this reason the management of such business and SLA driven settings has been so far not addressed considering real production requirements but only on the level of demonstrators.

The proposed framework in this thesis is aligned with the VO Model of Next Generation Grids and is based on the requirements for management of more then 20 application scenarios of Business Oriented Grid applications and is prepared with its goal to automate the management within service providers also for the increasing number of nodes for computing systems and the expected more complex hybrid computing systems in the next years.

Additionally the framework supports the necessary integration between the low level hardware management driven by performance metrics and the business viewpoint where more global goals and priorities are set that are supposed to be the ultimate drivers of the overall operation of resources and services.

7.1 Future work

There are many areas where future work could be based on the results presented here. An obvious domain for future work is to apply the presented management concept to different domains outside the provision of HPC utility service providers.

7.1.1 Modelling Support to feed the various Knowledge Bases

The framework relies on each layer on existing knowledge bases or rules. There is no prescribed format for these rules, policies or Ontologies as their concrete form is not relevant for the overall concept. However in practice the definition of these rules would require on one hand expert knowledge in the problem domain such as the administration of High-End resources and on the same time in depth understanding of the specific format of the knowledge base. The same problem applies to all levels in the management hierarchy.

Potential future work could aim to deliver a modelling tool supporting this knowledge engineering process necessary. Such a tool could be based on a modelling framework allowing the domain experts from the technical up to the business level to model their knowledge in descriptive diagrams leading to a kind of semi-formal description of their knowledge that could build the basis for the generation of formal Ontologies.

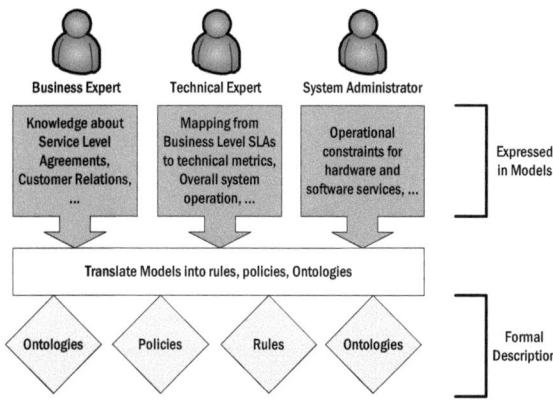

Figure 7.1: Knowledge Engineering Approach

As such a supporting tool is dependent itself from an appropriate configuration in the translation process a feedback and validation process would be necessary to allow an evolution of this mapping.

7.1.2 Supporting coupled applications on hybrid computing systems

For the HPC utility provider scenario it has been assumed that the execution of the job on the computational resources is not subject of control and management by the framework but that the responsibilities are limited to ensure a proper execution environment for them.

Considering the trend towards the virtualization of cluster systems allowing a dynamic partitioning of the resources and the movement away from computing systems realised using one single

Chapter 7 Conclusion and Outlook

type of processor towards hybrid systems one could imagine the application of the local management concept of the framework for supporting the interaction of the applications with the underlying compute environment and to dynamically change and adapt the coupled application configuration.

As significantly different timing constraints need to be considered the manageability layer would not be based on XML based common information layers and also the management modules would need to be realised not by exploiting external knowledge bases for their decisions. A potential realisation of such a scenario could be to allow the applications to be executed on the most appropriate architecture within the hybrid computing system and communicating all necessary data exchanges with the other applications in the usual way using for example Message Passing Interface (MPI). Additionally these applications would need to communicate pre-defined events towards an application manager component that is running within the hybrid computing system and that had been launched simultaneously together with this group of coupled applications. This pre-defined events could indicate increased or decreased demands on compute resources, disk resources, ... requesting an update of the configuration for example by increasing/decreasing the number of available virtualized instances. Beyond this one could imagine an update of the configuration of the locally distributed applications by launching another application covering other aspects of the model necessary as some properties e.g. behaviour of material is changing dramatically.

In order to integrate such an application manager within the overall management concept first of all the application manager could communicate similarly to all other components the taken decisions as incident reports and could also be instrumented to accept external commands (e.g. cancel the application). In order not to loose the advantages of the external knowledge base updates one could split the preparation of the application manager operation and the actual execution. In this sense the modelling of the different roles and the interactions of the different applications would be done by the *Coupled Applications Designer*. This model together with the current knowledge bases for the application management layer (e.g. indicating boundaries for increase/decrease requests, ...) would lead to configuration files for the applications to support the anticipated events and commands and would generate the configuration for the application manager.

7.1.3 Standardisation of Incident Reports and Command formats

The disadvantage of a non-standardised format for the incident reports and commands would be similar to the problems discussed along the need for a common monitoring format. While CIM or GLUE are quite straightforward candidates for the common monitoring format there is no similar pre-dominating specification for the monitoring and command messages. The competing specifications in the Web Service domain defined by the Distributed Management Task Force (DMTF) in Web Based Enterprise Management (WBEM) and by Organization for the Advancement of Structured Information Standards (OASIS) with Management Using Web Services (MUWS) are both appropriate candidates but the lack of agreement in this domain prevents a model where the management layers could be implemented by different vendors. So in the case of the HPC Utility Provider one could imagine that the Local Management and Manageability Layer for the compute nodes is delivered together with the hardware system as an integral software part of the installation by the hardware vendor. If several hardware systems are operated by the HPC provider and the goal is to put similar to the considered scenario in the previous chapter on top of this local management an technical integration level coordinating all these resources from different vendors and similarly solutions for the access middleware a common message is clearly necessary.

Furthermore the highest layer proposed in the HPC utility scenario is dealing with customer relations, offering and maintaining Service Level Agreements and would not be within the field of expertise of a single hardware vendor and would more likely fit into the portfolio of large IT companies dealing with Customer Relationship Management (CRM) and/or Service Oriented Architecture (SOA) based service provision frameworks.

Consequently a standardisation of the cross layer communication would be necessary if the realisation of the different layers is expected to be provided by commercial vendors. With such a solution the HPC utility provider could focus on the maintenance of the various knowledge bases rather then on the development and integration of the different management layers.

7.1.4 Cross-layer communication and self-organizing approaches

The presented concept is strictly hierarchical and based on externally defined knowledge. While this approach has the advantage of clearly defined responsibilities and chain-of-command the danger of taking wrong decisions based on the local context is an obvious drawback. While this problem is addressed by the reporting of incidents to the higher layers with the possibility to overrule decisions comes together with a potentially longer decision time.

Additionally the system does not foresee an update of the knowledge bases within a layer but only driven by external commands coming from the outside, namely human operators or higher layers. It is not foreseen that the knowledge bases are updated automatically based on the experiences of applying certain measures or by following an agent like approach discussing potential options with other entities on the same level.

Chapter 7 Conclusion and Outlook

A potential extension of the concept would be to allow at least to evolve the knowledge bases autonomously within certain boundaries and to establish also communications across the layers moving from the strict tree structure towards a mesh or Peer-To-Peer topology. This would be particular interesting for the VO management part as the presence of a central VO Management entity is not always necessary for achieving the VO goals. The merge of agent based approaches, self-learning and self-adaptation mechanisms could improve the system but would also introduce the risk that based on the lack of authority decisions might take longer or in the extreme case cannot be taken at all. The above mentioned move towards the use of agents have been already taken up in the running research project *Business objective driven reliable and intelligent Grids for real business (BREIN)*[1] aiming to merge Agents, Semantics and Grid technology and is technically coordinated by the author of this thesis.

---

[1] http://www.eu-brein.com/

Bibliography

[1] I. Foster, C. Kesselman, and S. Tuecke, "The anatomy of the Grid: Enabling scalable virtual organizations," *Lecture Notes in Computer Science*, vol. 2150, 2001. (document), 1, 2.2, 4.1.2

[2] D. Erwin, H.-C. Hoppe, S. Wesner, M. Romberg, P. Weber, E. Krenzien, P. Lindner, A. Streit, H. Richter, H. Stüben, V. Huber, S. Haubold, and E. Gabriel, "Unicore plus final report," tech. rep., UNICORE Consortium, 2003. (document), 2.2, 2.3, 4.1.2.1

[3] "Deisa primer." http://www.deisa.org/files/DEISAPrimer-V1-1.pdf, 2005. (document), 1, 2.2, 2.3.1, 4.1.2.1

[4] J. Byrne, "The virtual corporation," *Business Week*, pp. 36–41, 1993. (document), 2.2

[5] R. Grenier and G. Metes, *Going virtual: Moving your organization into the 21st centruy*. Prentice Hall, 1995. (document), 2.2

[6] L. Wildeman, "Alliances and networks: the next generation," *Internation Journal of Technology Management*, vol. 15, pp. 96–108, 1998. (document), 2.2

[7] T. Strader, F. Lin, and M. Shaw, "Information structure for electronic virtual organization management," *Decision Support Systems*, vol. 23, pp. 75–94, 1998. (document), 2.2, 2.3.3

[8] J. van Aken, L. Hop, and G. Post, *Managing Strategically in an Interconnected World*, ch. The Virtual Organization: A Special Mode of Strong Interorganizational Cooperation. John Wiley & Sons, 1998. (document), 2.2

[9] N. Lethbridge, "An i-based taxonomy of virtual organisations and the implications for effective management," *Informing Science*, vol. 4, no. 1, pp. 17–24, 2001. (document), 2.2, 2.3.1.1

[10] G. Keller, M. Nüüttgens, and A.-W. Scheer, "Semantische prozeßmodellierung auf der grundlage ereignisgesteuerter prozeflketten (epk)," tech. rep., Institut f,r Wirtschaftsinformatik, 1992. (document), 1.1

[11] B. Katzy, "Design and implementation of virtual organisations," working paper series, University BW Munich, 1998. (document), 2.2, 2.7, 2.3.3

[12] M. L. Massie, B. N. Chun, and D. E. Culler, "The ganglia distributed monitoring system: Design, implementation, and experience." http://ganglia.sourceforge.net/

Bibliography

talks/parallel_computing/ganglia-twocol.pdf. (document), 4.2.7.7, 4.6, 6.1.1

[13] T. Röblitz et al., "Autonomic management of large clusters and their integration into the grid," *Journal of Grid computing*, vol. 2, pp. 247–260, September 2004. (document), 4.2.7.8, 4.7, 4.3.1, 5.2.1, 5.3, 5.3, 6.1.1

[14] S. Andreozzi, N. D. Bortoli, S. Fantinel, A. Ghiselli, G. L. Rubini, G. Tortone, and M. C. Vistoli, "Gridice: a monitoring service for grid systems.," *Future Generation Comp. Syst.*, vol. 21, no. 4, pp. 559–571, 2005. (document), 4.8, 4.2.7.10, 5.3

[15] "Unicore (uniform access over to internet to computing resources)." http://www.unicore.de. see also http://www.unicore.org. 1, 2.2, 2.3, 4.1.2.1

[16] "Sg voms guide." EGEE Deliverable. 1, 2.2, 2.3.1

[17] A. E. Arenas, I. Djordjevic, T. Dimitrakos, L. Titkov, J. Claessens, C. Geuer-Pollmann, E. C. Lupu, N. Tuptuk, S. Wesner, and L. Schubert, "Trust and security in virtual organisations," in *PRO-VE 2005*, 2005. 1, 1.3, 2.3

[18] L. Schubert, S. Wesner, and T. Dimitrakos, "Secure and dynamic virtual organizations for business," in *Innovation and the Knowledge Economy: Issues, Applications, Case Studies* (P. Cunningham and M. Cunningham, eds.), IOS Press Amsterdam, 2005. ISBN: 1-58603-563-0. 1, 1.3, 2.3, 2.3.3

[19] M. S. (Editor), "Nextgrid workpackage progress report," tech. rep., NextGrid Consortium, 2005. 1, 4.1.2.2

[20] S. Wesner, "Towards a mobile grid architecture," *IT Information Technology*, 2005. 1, 3.7

[21] C. Loos, S. Wesner, and J. M. Jähnert, "Specific challenges of mobile dynamic virtual organizations," in *Innovation and the Knowledge Economy: Issues, Applications, Case Studies* (P. Cunningham and M. Cunningham, eds.), IOS Press Amsterdam, 2005. 1, 1.3, 2.3.3

[22] S. Wesner, T. Dimitrakos, and K. Jefferey, "Akogrimo - the grid goes mobile," Tech. Rep. 59, ERCIM News No. 59, October 2004. 1

[23] C. Catlett and L. Smarr, "Metacomputing," *Communications ACM*, vol. 35, pp. 44–52, June 1992. 1

[24] I. Foster, C. Kesselman, J. Nick, and S. Tuecke, "The physiology of the grid: An open grid services architecture for distributed systems integration," tech. rep., Global Grid Forum. 1, 4.1, 4.1.2

[25] W3C, "Web services architecture," w3c working group note, W3C, February 2004. 1

Bibliography

[26] W. Andrews, R. Valdes, G. Phifer, R. Wagner, C. Abrams, D. M. Smith, M. Cantara, B. Pring, B. M. Caldwell, C. Haight, L. F. Kenney, and J. Duggan, "Predicts 2005: The impact of web services still grows," 2004. 1, 4.1.1

[27] S. Wesner, L. Schubert, and T. Dimitrakos, "Dynamic virtual organisations in engineering," 2005. 1.3, 2.3

[28] J. Vallés, T. Dimitrakos, S. Wesner, B. Serhan, and P. Ritrovato, "The grid for e-collaboration and virtual organisations," in *Building the Knowledge Economy: Issues, Applications, Case Studies* (P. Cunningham, M. Cunningham, and P. Fatelnig, eds.), IOS Press Amsterdam ISBN: 1-58603-379-4, 2003. 1.3, 2.3.3, 4.1.2.4

[29] T. Dimitrakos, G. Laria, I. Djordjevic, N. Romano, F. D'Andria, V. Trpkovski, P. Kearney, M. Gaeta, P. Ritrovato, L. Schubert, B. Serhan, L. Titkov, and S. Wesner, "Towards a grid platform enabling dynamic virtual organisations for business applications," in *iTrust* (P. Herrmann, V. Issarny, and S. Shiu, eds.), vol. 3477 of *Lecture Notes in Computer Science*, pp. 406–410, Springer, 2005. 1.3, 4.1.2.4

[30] S. Wesner, I. Müller, Y. Salop, and P. Douriaguine, "Genesys architecture," tech. rep., GeneSyS IST-2201-34162, 2003. 1.3, 4.2.7.3, 5.2.1, 5.2.2.2, 5.3

[31] B. P. abd A[ndrey] Sadovykh and S. Wesner, "Genesys: Innovative framework for comprehensive supervision in multiple domains," in *ICWI 2004*, pp. 596–603, 2004. 1.3, 3.6, 4.2.7.3, 5.3

[32] A. Sadovykh, S. Wesner, and J.-E. Bohdanowicz, "Genesys: A generic architecture for supervision of distributed applications," in *Euroweb 2002*, December 2002. 1.3, 3.6, 4.2.7.3, 5.2.2.2, 5.3

[33] J.-E. Bohdanowicz, L. Kovacs, B. P. abd Andrey Sadovykh, and S. Wesner, "On distributed system supervision - a modern approach: Genesys," in *Network Control and Engineering for QoS, Security and Mobility, IFIP TC6 Conference*, 2004. Palma de Mallorca, Spain - November, 2004. 1.3, 3.6, 4.2.7.3, 5.3

[34] J.-E. Bohdanowicz, S. Wesner, L. Kovacs, H. Heimer, and A. Sadovykh, "The problematic of distributed systems supervision - an example: Genesys," in *IFIP Congress Tutorials 2004*, pp. 115–150, 2004. 1.3, 3.6, 4.2.7.3, 5.3

[35] B. Katzy and M. Dissel, "A toolset for building the virtual enterprise," *Journal of Intelligent Manufacturing*, vol. 12, no. 2, pp. 121–131, 2001. 2.2, 2.3.2, 1, 2.3.2.1

[36] W. Saabeel, T. Verduijn, L. Hagdorn, and K. Kumar, "A model for virtual organisation: A structure and process perspective," *eJov*, vol. 4, pp. 1–16, 2002. 2.2, 2.3.1, 2.3.3

Bibliography

[37] K. Jefferey and D. Snelling, "Next generation grids 2," tech. rep., European Commission, 2004. 2.2

[38] R. T. (Editor), "Next generation grids," tech. rep., European Commission, 2003. 2.2

[39] M. Romberg, "The UNICORE architecture seamless access to distributed resources," in *High Performance Distributed Computing*, Aug. 1999. 2.2, 2.3, 4.1.2.1

[40] T. Dimitrakos, D. M. Randal, F. Yuan, M. Gaeta, G. Laria, P. Ritrovato, B. Serhan, S. Wesner, and K. Wulf, "An emerging architecture enabling grid based applicati-on service provision," in *7th IEEE International Enterprise Distributed Object Computing Conference EDOC 2003*, September 2003. Brisbane Australia, September 16-19 2003. 2.3, 4.1.2.4

[41] M. Gaeta, G. Laria, P. Ritrovato, N. Romano, B. Serhan, S. Wesner, T. Dimitrakos, and D. M. Randal, "Trust, security, and contract management challenges for grid-based application service provision," in *iTrust*, pp. 362–368, 2004. 2.3, 4.1.2.4

[42] T. Dimitrakos, D. Golby, and P. Kearney, "Towards a trust and contract management framework for dynamic virtual organisations," in *eAdoption and the Knowledge Economy: eChallenges 2004*, IOS Press, 2004. 2.3

[43] R. Wigand, A. Picot, and R. Reichwald, *Information, organisation and management: Expanding markets and corporate boundaries*. John Wiley & Sons, 1997. 2.3.1

[44] D. Jordan and J. Evdemon, "Web services business process execution language version 2.0," tech. rep., OASIS, 2006. 2.3.1.1

[45] N. Kavantzas, D. Burdett, G. Ritzinger, T. Fletcher, Y. Lafon, and C. Barreto, "Web services choreography description language version 1.0," tech. rep., W3C, 2005. 2.3.1.1

[46] W3C, "Web services description language (wsdl) 1.1," tech. rep., W3C Working Draft. 2.3.2.2, 4.1.2

[47] D. Martin, M. Burstein, J. Hobbs, O. Lassila, D. McDermott, S. McIlraith, S. Narayanan, M. Paolucci, B. Parsia, T. Payne, E. Sirin, N. Srinivasan, and K. Sycara, "Owl-s: Semantic markup for web services," tech. rep., W3C, 2004. 2.3.2.2

[48] P. Masche, P. Mckee, and B. Mitchell, "The increasing role of service level agreements in b2b systems.," in *WEBIST (2)* (J. A. M. Cordeiro, V. Pedrosa, B. Encarnação, and J. Filipe, eds.), pp. 123–126, INSTICC Press, 2006. 2.3.2.2

[49] F. D'Andria, J. Martrat, G. Laria, P. Ritrovato, and S. Wesner, "An enhanced strategy for sla management in the business context of new mobile dynamic vo," in *Exploiting the Knowledge Economy: Issues, Applications, Case Studies* (P. Cunningham and M. Cunningham, eds.), eChallenges 2006, IOS Press Amsterdam, 2006. 2.3.2.2, 17, 5.2.3

[50] B. Koller and L. Schubert, "Towards autonomous sla management using a proxy-like approach.," in *NODe/GSEM* (R. Hirschfeld, R. Kowalczyk, A. Polze, and M. Weske, eds.), vol. 69 of *LNI*, pp. 259–275, GI, 2005. 2.3.2.2

[51] P. Hasselmeyer, B. Koller, L. Schubert, and P. Wieder, "Towards sla-supported resource management.," in *HPCC* (M. Gerndt and D. Kranzlmüller, eds.), vol. 4208 of *Lecture Notes in Computer Science*, pp. 743–752, Springer, 2006. 2.3.2.2

[52] M. D. Wilson, A. Arenas, and L. Schubert, "Trustcom framework v4," tech. rep., TrustCoM Project, 2007. 2.3.2.4, 2.3.2.4, 5.2.2, 5.2.3

[53] L. Chen, V. Tan, F. Xu, A. Biller, P. Groth, S. Miles, J. Ibbotson, M. Luck, and L. Moreau, "A proof of concept: Provenance in a service oriented architecture," in *4th UK eScience All Hands Meeting*, 2005. 2.3.2.4

[54] L. Camarinha-Matos and H. Afsarmanesh, "A roadmap for strategic research on virtual organizations," 2003. 2.3.3

[55] K. Petropoulos *et al.*, "D1.3 conceptual model of the laura prototype - definition of functionalities," tech. rep., LAURA IST Project, 2003. 2.3.3

[56] S. Wesner and A. Kipp, "Report on be classification and recommendations for architecture and interoperability," tech. rep., BEinGRID, 2007. 3.1, 3.4.2, 10

[57] A. Kipp, S. Wesner, H. Schwichtenberg, C. Thomson, and K. Dolkas, "Report on classification of grid solutions," tech. rep., BEinGRID, 2006. 3.1, 3.4.1, 3.4.2

[58] B. Dillaway, M. Humphrey, C. Smith, M. Theimer, and G. Wasson, "Hpc basic profile, version 1.0," tech. rep., OGF, 2007. 3.2

[59] A. Anjomshoaa, F. Brisard, M. Drescher, D. Fellows, A. Ly, S. McGough, D. Pulsipher, and A. Savva, "Job submission description language (jsdl) specification, version 1.0," tech. rep., OGF, 2006. 3.2

[60] I. Foster, A. Grimshaw, P. Lane, W. Lee, M. Morgan, S. Newhouse, S. Pickles, D. Pulsipher, C. Smith, and M. Theimer, "Ogsa basic execution service version 1.0," tech. rep., OGF, 2007. 3.2

[61] P. M. A. Sloot, C. A. Boucher, M. T. Bubak, A. G. Hoekstra, P. Plaszczak, A. Posthumus, D. van de Vijver, S. Wesner, and A. Tirado-Ramos, "VIROLAB - A virtual laboratory for decision support in viral diseases treatment," in *Cracow Grid Workshop 2005*, (Cracow, Poland), Nov. 2005. in press, best poster award. 3.5, 3.5.1

[62] E. C. Kaletas, H. Afsarmanesh, and L. O. Hertzberger, "A methodology for integrating new sci-

entific domains and applications in a virtual laboratory environment.," in *ICEIS (3)*, pp. 265–272, 2004. 3.5

[63] B. Kryza, R. Slota, M. Majewska, J. Pieczykolan, and J. Kitowski, "Grid organizational memory-provision of a high-level grid abstraction layer supported by ontology alignment," *Future Gener. Comput. Syst.*, vol. 23, no. 3, pp. 348–358, 2007. 3.5, 4.1.2

[64] P. N. (Editor), "D3.2 design of the virtual laboratory," tech. rep., Virolab Consortium, 2007. 3.5.1, 4.1.2.2

[65] D. Michel, H. Zunker, and R. Stoy, "Distributed interactive simulations on atm networks for space systems validation," in *Data Systems in Aerospace-DASIA Athens, 25.-28.Mai 1998*, pp. 1–8, 1998. LIDO-Berichtsjahr=1999,;. 3.6

[66] E. Frizziero, M. Gulmini, F. Lelli, G. Maron, A. Oh, S. Orlando, A. Petrucci, S. Squizzato, and S. Traldi, "Instrument element: A new grid component that enables the control of remote instrumentation.," in *CCGRID*, p. 52, IEEE Computer Society, 2006. 3.6

[67] M. Okon, D. Kaliszan, M. Lawenda, D. Stoklosa, T. Rajtar, N. Meyer, and M. Stroinski, "Virtual laboratory as a remote and interactive access to the scientific instrumentation embedded in grid environment," *e-science*, vol. 0, p. 124, 2006. 3.6

[68] J. Wedwik, B. Viken, S. Wesner, R. Piotter, I. Müller, T. Dimitrakos, G. Laria, C. Morariu, N. Inacio, P. Mandic, R. del Campo, and S. F. Gonzales, "The state of the art of mobile grids," tech. rep., Akogrimo consortium, 2005. 3.7

[69] H. Kreger, "Web services conceptual architecture," tech. rep., IBM, 2001. 4.1, 4.1.1

[70] "Anatomy of the client/server model." http://edocs.bea.com/tuxedo/tux71/html/intbas3.htm. 4.1.1

[71] C. Longbottom, "Soa: Substance or hype?." http://www.quocirca.com/pages/analysis/reports/view/dl/store250/item1542/, 2006. 4.1.1

[72] D. Szubert and C. Longbottom, "Information and soa." http://www.quocirca.com/pages/analysis/reports/view/dl/store250/item3749/, 2007. 4.1.1

[73] "Web services addressing (ws-addressing)," tech. rep., W3C, 2004. 4.1.1

[74] A. Nadalin, C. Kaler, P. Hallam-Baker, and R. Monzillo, "Web services security: Soap message security 1.0," tech. rep., OASIS, 2004. 4.1.1

[75] S. Weerawarana, F. Curbera, F. Leymann, T. Storey, and D. F. Ferguson, *Web Services Platform Architecture : SOAP, WSDL, WS-Policy, WS-Addressing, WS-BPEL, WS-Reliable Messaging, and More*. Prentice Hall PTR, March 2005. 4.1.1

[76] S. Tuecke, K. Czajkowski, I. Foster, J. Frey, S. Graham, and C. Kesselman, "Grid service specification," tech. rep., Open Grid Service Infrastructure WG, Global Grid Forum. 4.1.2, 4.1.2.4

[77] R. T. Fielding, *Architectural Styles and the Design of Network-based Software Architectures*. PhD thesis, University of California, Irvine, 2000. 4.1.2

[78] R. Khare and R. N. Taylor, "Extending the representational state transfer (rest) architectural style for decentralized systems," in *ICSE '04: Proceedings of the 26th International Conference on Software Engineering*, (Washington, DC, USA), pp. 428–437, IEEE Computer Society, 2004. 4.1.2

[79] W. working group, "Web services for management (ws-management)," tech. rep., DMTF, 2006. 4.1.2, 4.2.7.5

[80] A. Hoheisel and U. Der, "An xml-based framework for loosely coupled applications on grid environments," in *International Conference on Computational Science* (P. M. A. Sloot, D. Abramson, A. V. Bogdanov, J. Dongarra, A. Y. Zomaya, and Y. E. Gorbachev, eds.), vol. 2657 of *Lecture Notes in Computer Science*, pp. 245–254, Springer, 2003. 4.1.2

[81] T. Fahringer, A. Jugravu, S. Pllana, R. Prodan, C. S. Junior, and H.-L. Truong, "ASKALON: A Tool Set for Cluster and Grid Computing," *Concurrency and Computation: Practice and Experience*, vol. 17, no. 2-4, 2005. http://dps.uibk.ac.at/askalon/. 4.1.2

[82] D. Snelling, "The abstract job object: An open framework for seamless computing." http://www.fz-juelich.de/unicoreplus/. 4.1.2.1

[83] J. Almond and D. Snelling, "Unicore: uniform access to supercomputing as an element of electronic commerce," in *FGCS Volume 15 (1999), Numbers 5-6*, vol. 15 of *FGCS*, pp. 539–548, 1999. 4.1.2.1

[84] D. Erwin, "Uniform interface to grid services." ftp://ftp.cordis.europa.eu/pub/ist/docs/grids/unigrids-interim-sheet_en.pdf. 4.1.2.1

[85] A. Dunlop, "Omii europe - an overview." http://152.78.70.96/OMII-Europe/News/OMII-Europe-Narr.pdf, 2005. 4.1.2.1

[86] F. Gagliardi, B. Jones, and E. Laure, "The EU DataGrid Project: Building and Operating a large scale Grid Infrastructure," in *Engineering the Grid: Status and Perspective* (B. Di Martino, J. Dongarra, A. Hoisie, L. Yang, and H. Zima, eds.), American Scientific Publishers, January 2006. 4.1.2.2, 4.1.2.3

[87] M. Assel, B. Krammer, and A. Loehden, "Management and access of biomedical data in a grid environment," in *Proceedings of the 6th Cracow Grid Workshop 2006, Oct. 15-18, 2006*,

Bibliography

Krakow, Poland (M. Bubak, M. Turala, and K. Wiatr, eds.), pp. 263–270, ACC Cyfronet AGH, 2007. 4.1.2.2

[88] E. Laure, F. Hemmer, F. Prelz, S. Beco, S. Fisher, M. Livny, L. Guy, M. Barroso, P. Buncic, P. Z. Kunszt, A. Di Meglio, A. Aimar, A. Edlund, D. Groep, F. Pacini, M. Sgaravatto, and O. Mulmo, "Middleware for the next generation grid infrastructure," no. EGEE-PUB-2004-002, p. 4 p, 2004. 4.1.2.3

[89] E. Laure, S. M. Fisher, A. Frohner, C. Grandi, P. Z. Kunszt, A. Krenek, O. Mulmo, F. Pacini, F. Prelz, J. White, M. Barroso, P. Buncic, F. Hemmer, A. Di Meglio, and A. Edlund, "Programming the grid with glite," Tech. Rep. EGEE-TR-2006-001, CERN, Geneva, Mar 2006. 4.1.2.3

[90] S. Wesner, B. Serhan, T. Dimitrakos, D. M. Randal, P. Ritrovato, and G. Laria, "Overview of an architecture enabling grid based application service provision," in *European Across Grids Conference*, pp. 113–118, 2004. 4.1.2.4

[91] S. Wesner, L. Schubert, T. Dimitrakos, D. M. Randal, M. Gaeta, P. Ritrovato, and G. Laria, "Towards a platform enabling grid based application service provision," in *eAdoption and the Knowledge Economy: Issues, Applications, Case Studies* (P. Cunningham and M. Cunningham, eds.), IOS Press Amsterdam, 2004. ISBN: 1-58603-470-7. 4.1.2.4, 5.2.3

[92] S. Andreozzi, S. Burke, L. Field, S. Fisher, B. Konya, M. Mambelli, J. M. Schopf, M. Viljoen, and A. Wilson, "Glue schema specification version 1.2," 2005. 4.2.1

[93] S. Andreozzi, S. Burke, F. Ehm, L. Field, G. Galang, B. Konya, M. Litmaath, P. Millar, and J. Navarro, "Glue specification v. 2.0 (draft)," tech. rep., OGF, GLUE WG, 2008. 4.2.1, 5.3

[94] L. Field, "Use cases for glue 2.0," tech. rep., GLUE-WG, OGF, 2008. 4.2.1

[95] "Itu-t recommendation x.711," tech. rep., ITU, 1997. 4.2.4

[96] M. Gering, "Comparison of snmp and cmip management architectures," pp. 197–216, 1994. 4.2.4

[97] U. S. Warrier, L. Besaw, L. LaBarre, and B. D. Handspicker, "RFC 1189: Common Management Information Services and Protocols for the Internet (CMOT and CMIP)," Oct. 1990. Obsoletes RFC1095 [130]. Status: HISTORIC. 4.2.4

[98] "Cim concepts white paper," tech. rep., DMTF, 2003. 4.2.5

[99] G. Rackl, *Monitoring and Managing Heterogenous Middleware*. PhD thesis, Institut f,r Informatik, Lehrstuhl f,r Rechnertechnik und Rechnerorganisation, 2001. 4.2.6, 5.3

[100] P. Drum and G. Rackl, "Applying and monitoring latency-based metacomputing infrastructures," in *Proceedings of the 2000 International Workshops on Parallel Processing*, IEEE, 2000. 4.2.6

Bibliography

[101] B. Tierney, R. Aydt, D. Gunter, W. Smith, V. Taylor, and R. W. an M. Swany, "A grid monitoring architecture," 2002. 4.2.7

[102] R. L. Ribler, H. Simitci, and D. A. Reed, "The autopilot performance-directed adaptive control system," 1997. 4.2.7

[103] B. Tierney, B. Crowley, D. Gunter, M. Holding, J. Lee, and M. Thompson, "A monitoring sensor management system for grid environments," in *HPDC '00: Proceedings of the 9th IEEE International Symposium on High Performance Distributed Computing*, (Washington, DC, USA), p. 97, IEEE Computer Society, 2000. 4.2.7

[104] A. Waheed, W. Smith, J. George, and J. C. Yan, "An infrastructure for monitoring and management in computational grids," in *LCR '00: Selected Papers from the 5th International Workshop on Languages, Compilers, and Run-Time Systems for Scalable Computers*, (London, UK), pp. 235–245, Springer-Verlag, 2000. 4.2.7

[105] R. Wolski, N. Spring, and J. Hayes, "The Network Weather Service: A Distributed Resource Performance Forecasting Service for Metacomputing," *Journal of Future Generation Computing Systems*, vol. 15, pp. 757–768, 1999. 4.2.7

[106] A. Cooke, A. Gray, W. Nutt, J. Magowan, M. Oevers, P. Taylor, R. Cordenonsi, R. Byrom, L. Cornwall, A. Djaoui, L. Field, S. Fisher, S. Hicks, J. Leake, R. Middleton, A. Wilson, X. Zhu, N. Podhorszki, B. Coghlan, S. Kenny, D. O'Callaghan, and J. Ryan, "The relational grid monitoring architecture: Mediating information about the grid." 4.2.7.1

[107] A. Keller and H. Ludwig, "Defining and monitoring service level agreements for dynamic e-business," 2002. 4.2.7.2, 5.2.3

[108] H. Kreger, V. Bullard, and W. Vambenepe, "Web services distributed management: Management using web services (muws 1.1)," tech. rep., OASIS, 2006. 4.2.7.4

[109] B. Murray, K. Wilson, and M. Ellison, "Web services distributed management: Muws primer," tech. rep., OASIS, 2006. 4.2.7.4

[110] S. Velt, "Neues vom schutzheiligen: Nagios in version 3.0 freigegeben," tech. rep., IX, 2008. 4.2.7.6, 5.2.1, 5.3, 6.1.1

[111] K. Hätinen, M. Klemettinen, and M. H., "Knowledge discovery from telecommunication network alarm databases," in *International Conference on Data Engineering (ICDE'96)*, pp. 115–122, 1996. 4.3.1

[112] L. Lewis, "A case-based reasoning approach to the resolution of faults in communication networks," in *Integrated Network Management III*, pp. 671–682, 1993. 4.3.1

137

Bibliography

[113] G. D. Rodosek, *A Framework for Supporting Fault Diagnosis in Integrated Network and Systems Management: Methodologies for the Correlation of Trouble Tickets and Access to Problem-Solving Expertise*. PhD thesis, Ludwig-Maximilians-Universit%ot M¸nchen, 1995. 4.3.1

[114] B. Gruschke, "Integrated event management: Event correlation using dependency graphs," in *Network Operations and Management Symposium DSOM1998*, 1998. 4.3.1

[115] R. Gardner and D. Harle, "Pattern discovery and specfication translation for alarm correlation," in *Netowrk Operations and Management Symposium (NOMS1998)*, pp. 713–722, 1998. 4.3.1

[116] P. Wu, R. Bhatnagar, L. Epshtein, *et al.*, "Alarm correlation engine (ace)," in *Network Operations and Management Symposium (NOMS1998)*, pp. 733–742, 1998. 4.3.1

[117] D. Ohsie, A. Mayer, S. Kliger, *et al.*, "Event modeling with the model language," in *Integrated Network Management V (IM97)* (R. S. A. Lazar and R. Stadler, eds.), pp. 625–637, 1997. 4.3.1

[118] N. C. Damianou, *A Policy Framework for Management of Distributed Systems*. PhD thesis, Imperial College of Science, Technology and Medicine University of London Department of Computing, 2002. 4.3.2

[119] B. Moore, E. Ellesson, J. Strassner, and A. Westerinen, "Policy core information model." available at: http://www.faqs.org/rfcs/rfc3060.html, Feb 2001. 4.3.2

[120] N. Damianou, N. Dulay, E. Lupu, and M. Sloman, "The ponder policy specification language," *Lecture Notes in Computer Science*, vol. 1995, pp. 18–??, 2001. 4.3.2

[121] L. Kagal, T. Finin, and A. Joshi, "A Policy Language for A Pervasive Computing Environment," in *4th International Workshop on Policies for Distributed Systems and Networks*, IEEE, June 2003. 4.3.2

[122] V. Danciu, *Application of policy-based techniques to process-oriented IT service management*. PhD thesis, Fakultät für Mathematik, Informatik und Statistik der Ludwig-Maximilians-Universität München, 2007. 4.3.2

[123] T. Moses, "extensible access control markup language (xacml) version 2.0," tech. rep., OASIS Standard, 2005. 4.3.2

[124] I. Aib, M. Sallé, C. Bartolini, A. Boulmakoul, R. Boutaba, and G. Pujolle, "Business aware policy based management," tech. rep., HP, 2005. 4.4

[125] E. Imamagic and D. Dobrenic, "Grid infrastructure monitoring system based on nagios," in *GMW '07: Proceedings of the 2007 workshop on Grid monitoring*, (New York, NY, USA), pp. 23–28, ACM, 2007. 5.2.1

[126] J. M. Jähnert, S. Wesner, and V. A. Villagrá, "The akogrimo mobile grid reference architecture - overview," tech. rep., Akogrimo, 2007. 5.2.2, 5.2.3

[127] S. Smallen, C. Olschanowsky, K. Ericson, P. Beckman, and J. M. Schopf, "The inca test harness and reporting framework," in *Supercomputing Conference*, 2004. 5.3, 5.3

[128] J. Case, M. Fedor, M. Schoffstall, and J. Davin, "Simple network management protocol," tech. rep., IETF, 1990. 6.1.1

[129] A. Andrieux *et al.*, "Web services agreement specification," tech. rep., OASIS, 2005. 6.1.4

[130] U. S. Warrier and L. Besaw, "Common management information services and protocol over tcp/ip (cmot)," 1989. 97

Bibliography

Index

Business Relation Management, 106, 118

CIM, 63
CMIP, 63

DMI, 62

GANGLIA, 108
Ganglia, 70
GeneSyS, 29, 47, 67
GLUE, 61
GMA, 65
Grid
    Akogrimo, 29, 49
    BEinGRID, 29
    DataGrid, 59
    DEISA, 9
    EGEE, 9
    gLite, 59
    Globus, 58
    GRASP, 29, 59
    GRIA, 60
    GridCC, 47
    K-WF Grid, 44
    NextGrid, 29
    RinGrid, 47
    UNICORE, 9, 57, 105
    VIROLAB, 44
Grid Computing, 56
GridICE, 72

INCA, 72

JSDL, 30

Lemon, 71, 108
Local Management, 106, 109

manageability, 108
Mediator, 122
MIMO, 65
MUWS, 69

Nagios, 70, 108
Network Management, 108

OGSA, 56

Policy Based Management, 75

Resource Management, 106

Service Broker, 54
Service Level Agreement, 3, 37, 51, 60, 66, 81, 105, 119, 120
Service Management, 112
Service Oriented Architecture, 53
Service Provider, 54
    GRASP, 35
    Core Service Provider, 30
Simple Network Management Protocol, 62
SNMP, 108
SOA, 53
standard
    HPC Basic Profile, 30
    JSDL, 30
    OGSA-BES, 30

TrustCoM, 9, 29

UNICORE, 111

Virtual Organisation, 7, 9
    lifecycle, 24, 32
    role model, 16

    structure, 13
    topology, 13, 103

WSDL, 71
WSLA, 66

Abbreviations

AgSP (Aggregated Service Provision) , p. 35.
AJO (Abstract Job Object) , p. 16.
Akogrimo (Access to Knowledge through the Grid in a Mobile World) , p. 6.
API (Application Programmer Interface) , p. 70.
ASP (Application Service Provision) , p. 2.
B2B (Business to Business) , p. 13.
BEinGRID (Business Experiments in Grids) , p. 6.
BES (Basic Execution Service) , p. 30.
BPEL (Business Process Execution Language) , p. 14.
BREIN (Business objective driven reliable and intelligent Grids for real business) , p. 128.
CAVE (Cave Automatic Virtual Environment) , p. 50.
CBD (Component Based Development) , p. 54.
CIM (Component Information Model) , p. 3.
CMIP (Common Management Information Protocol) , p. 62.
CMIPM (CMIP Machine) , p. 63.
CMOT (CMIP over TCP/IP) , p. 63.
CMS (Content Management System) , p. 30.
CORBA (Common Object Request Broker) , p. 54.
CRM (Customer Relationship Management) , p. 104.
DAG (Directed Acyclic Graph) , p. 14.
DCOM (Distributed Component Object Model) , p. 54.
DEISA (Distributed European Infrastructure for Supercomputer Applications) , p. i.
DMI (Desktop Management Interface) , p. 62.
DMTF (Distributed Management Task Force) , p. 63.
EDI (Electronic Data Interchange) , p. 56.
EGEE (Enabling Grids for E-Science) , p. 1.

ABBREVIATIONS

ELeGI (European Learning Grid Infrastructure), p. 6.
EMS (Execution Management Service), p. 30.
EN (Enterprise Network), p. 23.
EPC (Event driven process chain), p. xiii.
FDR (Fault Detection and Recovery), p. 69.
GeneSyS (Generic System Supervision), p. 6.
Globus (Globus Toolkit), p. 58.
GLUE (Grid Laboratory Uniform Environment), p. 61.
GMA (Grid Monitoring Architecture), p. 64.
GOC (Grid Operations Centre), p. 71.
GRASP (Grid based Application Service Provision), p. 6.
GRIA (Grid for Industrial Applications), p. 60.
Grid computational infrastructure (Grid), p. 2.
GridCC (Grid Enabled Remote Instrumentation with Distribtued Control and Computation), p. 47.
HPC (High Performance Computing), p. i.
IDB (Incarnation Database), p. 57.
IETF (Internet Engineering Task Force), p. 61.
IP (Internet Protocol), p. 86.
J2EE (Java 2 Enterprise Edition), p. 55.
Java (The Java Toolkit), p. 58.
JMX (Java Management Extensions), p. 83.
JSDL (Job Service Description Language), p. 30.
K-Wf Grid (Knowledge based Worflow Systems for Grid Applications), p. 44.
KB (Knowledge Base), p. 110.
MDS (Meta Directory Service), p. 71.
MIB (Management Information Base), p. 3.
MOM (Message Oriented Middleware), p. 55.
MPI (Message Passing Interface), p. 58.
MUWS (Management Using Web Services), p. 65.
NextGrid (The Next Generation Grid), p. 29.
NGG (Next Generation Grids), p. 9.
NJS (Network Job Supervisor), p. 57.
NRPE (Nagios Remote Plug-In Executor), p. 68.

ABBREVIATIONS

OASIS (Organization for the Advancement of Structured Information Standards) , p. 56.
OGSA (Open Grid Service Architecture) , p. 30.
OGSA-DAI (Open Grid Service Architecture-Data Access and Integration) , p. 59.
OGSI (Open Grid Service Infrastructure) , p. 56.
OLAP (On-Line Analytical Processing) , p. 72.
OO (Object Orientation) , p. 54.
Open Grid Forum (OGF) , p. 30.
OSI (Open Systems Interconnection) , p. 63.
OWL-S (Semantic Markup for Web Services) , p. 18.
P2P (Peer-to-Peer Computing) , p. 29.
PBM (Policy based Management) , p. ii.
PDP (Policy Decision Point) , p. 74.
PEP (Policy Enforcement Point) , p. 74.
PKI (Public Key Infrastructure) , p. 60.
QoS (Quality of Service) , p. 2.
R-GMA (Relational Grid Monitoring Architecture) , p. 64.
REST (Representational State Transfer) , p. 56.
RinGrid (Remote Instrumentation on Next Generation Grids) , p. 47.
RPC (Remote Procedure Call) , p. 54.
RTI (Run-Time-Infrastructure) , p. 47.
SAML (Security Asstertion Markup Language) , p. 58.
SBI (Service Based Infrastructures) , p. 2.
SIMDAT (Grids for Industrial Product Development) , p. 60.
SLA (Service Level Agreement) , p. 2.
SLO (Service Level Objectives) , p. 3.
SME (Small and Medium Enterprise) , p. 39.
SMS (Short Message Service) , p. 72.
SNMP (Simple Network Management Protocol) , p. 3.
SOA (Service Oriented Architecture) , p. i.
SSH (Secure Shell) , p. 103.
TCP (Transport Control Protocol) , p. 70.
TrustCoM (Trust and Contract Management Framework) , p. 6.
TSI (Target System Interface) , p. 57.

ABBREVIATIONS

TTP (Trusted Third Party) , p. 18.
UDDI (Universal Directory and Discovery Interface) , p. 40.
UDP (User Datagram Protocol) , p. 70.
UML (Unified Modeling Language) , p. 63.
UMTS (Universal Mobile Communication System) , p. 49.
UNICORE (Uniform Access over the Internet to Computing Resources) , p. i.
VBE (Virtual Breeding Environment) , p. 40.
VHE (Virtual Hosting Environment) , p. 60.
VIROLAB (A virtual laboratory for decision support in viral diseases treatment) , p. 44.
VL-E (Virtual Laboratory for eScience) , p. 44.
VO (Virtual Organisation) , p. i.
WBEM (Web Based Enterprise Management) , p. 68.
WLAN (Wireless Local Area Access Network) , p. 38.
WMI (Windows Management Interface) , p. 3.
WS-CDL (Web Service Choreography Definition Language) , p. 14.
WS-RF (Web Service Resource Framework) , p. 56.
WSDL (Web Service Description Language) , p. 18.
WSDM (Web Service Distributed Management) , p. 67.
WSLA (Web Service Level Agreement) , p. 65.
WSRF (Web Service Resource Framework) , p. 67.
XACML (eXtensible Access Control Modeling Language) , p. 75.
XML (eXtensible Meta Language) , p. 65.

Die VDM Verlagsservicegesellschaft sucht für wissenschaftliche Verlage abgeschlossene und herausragende

Dissertationen, Habilitationen, Diplomarbeiten, Master Theses, Magisterarbeiten usw.

für die kostenlose Publikation als Fachbuch.

Sie verfügen über eine Arbeit, die hohen inhaltlichen und formalen Ansprüchen genügt, und haben Interesse an einer honorarvergüteten Publikation?

Dann senden Sie bitte erste Informationen über sich und Ihre Arbeit per Email an *info@vdm-vsg.de*.

Sie erhalten kurzfristig unser Feedback!

VDM Verlagsservicegesellschaft mbH
Dudweiler Landstr. 99   Telefon +49 681 3720 174
D - 66123 Saarbrücken   Fax   +49 681 3720 1749
www.vdm-vsg.de

Die VDM Verlagsservicegesellschaft mbH vertritt

Printed by Books on Demand GmbH, Norderstedt / Germany